2495

EVERYTHING YOU NEED TO K

# SCOOTERS

ERIC DREGNI,
WITH PHOTOGRAPHY BY PIXEL PETE

**MOTORBOOKS**

## DEDICATION

For Tim and all his scootering advice and humor—especially when we were elbow-deep in grease in my parents' garage and the devout from St. Luke's came to a potluck bearing hotdishes and asked what the heck we were doing with our lives.

## ACKNOWLEDMENTS

Eilifinissimo; fratello mio Michael Dregni; Paolo Giuri for sneaking me into la Piaggio in spite of impending strikes; Stephen "Stefano" Heller; Jim Kilau for his continual hunt for the most obscure American scooters; Hans Kruger and his scooter museum auf Deutschland; P. K. McCarthy, of course; Willy and Sam Niskanen; Jonathan Ogilvy; the regular Regulars; Bob (and Derrick) at Scooterville for bringing affordable scooters back into town; Vittorio Tessera and his golden-fleeced Lambretta; Pete "I Don't Know Anything about Scooters" Townshend; Becky "Beks" Wallace; and Jeremy Wilker.

Finally, many, many thank-yous go out to the dedicated scooter owners, collectors, and clubs whose lovingly-restored and well-maintained scooters appear throughout this book.

First published in 2005 by Motorbooks, an imprint of MBI Publishing Company, Galtier Plaza, Suite 200, 380 Jackson Street, St. Paul, MN 55101-3885 USA

MBI Publishing Company titles are also available at discounts in bulk quantity for industrial or sales-promotional use. For details write to Special Sales Manager at MBI Publishing Company, Galtier Plaza, Suite 200, 380 Jackson Street, St. Paul, MN 55101-3885 USA.

ISBN-10: 0-7603-2217-1
ISBN-13: 978-0-7603-2217-8

**Front Cover:** This Scarabeo (and its rider) is fully equipped for long-distance traveling.

**Frontispiece:** Kent Aldrich's classically mod Stella may have room for one more mirror, but not likely.

**Back cover: (top)** These two slick modsters are ready for any adventure their Stella can throw at them.

**(bottom)** The Suzuki Burgman is part of the modern family of maxi-scooters. Its 638cc engine is more than enough to carry itself at speed down the freeway.

**About the author:** Eric Dregni first discovered the sleek beauty of Lambretta scooters while living in Brescia, Italy. Having been transformed by the light, he moved closer to the Innocenti factory in the Lambrate quarter of Milan, which had also become a pilgrimage site for transvestites from across the continent. Dregni traveled around Europe and the U.S. visiting scooter museums, factories, and meeting with collectors and clubs. He is the author of five other scooter books (three of them written with his brother Michael) including The Illustrated MotorScooter Buyer's Guide, Scooters!, Scooter Mania, and The Scooter Bible.

Editor: Peter Schletty
Designer: Brenda C. Canales

Printed in China

# CONTENTS

# SCOOTER HISTORY

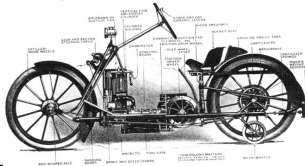

THE "MILITAIRE" is built in *anticipation* of the logical evolution of the motorcycle. It is the result of keen study of traffic and other conditions in this country, and we unhesitatingly affirm that the "MILITAIRE" is better fitted to cope with road conditions than any other motorcycle on the market. It is radical, we admit, but so was Fulton's steamboat, and Marconi's wireless, and Westinghouse's brake.

*Give yourself a chance to learn more about*

## The "Militaire"

THE MILITAIRE AUTO CO. (Inc.) CLEVELAND OHIO

---

## WHAT YOU WILL LEARN

- Scooters evolved from a motorized skateboard to the Vespa
- The first motorcycle was a scooter!
- The five commandments by which all scooters must abide
- How Moto Scoots survived Al Capone's Chicago
- Owning a Vespa prevents you from becoming a Communist
- How the maker of Japanese kamikaze planes switched to scooter production

---

### 1912 Militaire

The American Militaire was part motorscooter, part motorcycle, and part Jules Verne spaceship, a far-out vision of the future in the pioneering days of motorized vehicles. Note the Militaire's artillery wood wheels, open-to-the-elements steering gears, shock absorber, bucket seat, rider's height adjuster, and the idler wheels that could be lowered while waiting at America's first electric traffic signal, erected in Cleveland in 1914.

Cities in the 1800s were in sorry shape. Horses were the mainstay of transportation around the turn of the century, and during rush hour they would often drop dead from overexertion. When sharpened spurs failed to coax tired steeds, teamsters supposedly would light fires under horses' bellies to urge them up hills.

Luckily, the noble and eccentric Baron Drais of Karlsruhe, Germany, knew that necessity breeds invention and had been hard at work in his workshop to mobilize the world. He scorned the life of luxury and followed his lust for inventing, unveiling a vehicle that would revolutionize the world in 1813. He started with the correct notion that a walking man uses up too much energy by throwing about his weight from one foot to the other. "How is it possible to keep one's body constantly in the same axis when moving forward?" asked Egon Larsen in *Ideas and Invention*.

After he proved to the naysayers from his town that he could easily wheel from Karlsruhe to the neighboring town in less than half the time it took by foot, he was allowed to patent his "velocipede"—but only in the province of Baden. His idea was soon picked up and copied across France, England, and the United States, where plagiarists avoided paying royalties by hiding their inventions behind pseudonyms like "dandy horses," "hobby horses," and "bone shakers." These early bicycles were considered playthings for the wealthy and were the butt of working-class jokes, especially the "penny-farthings" bikes, so called for the uneven relation of the front to back wheels.

As bicycles became the rage of the rich, Parisian inventor Jean-Joseph Lenoir made the very first internal combustion engine in 1860. Gottlieb Daimler and Nikolas Otto took Lenoir's motor to a new level by making it a four-stroke capable of 700 rpm, and in 1885, Daimler put it on one of Drais' velocipedes and the first gas-engine-powered motorcycle (with many

scooter-like qualities) was invented. After many attempts at wedging bulky steam engines into a velocipede frame in Italy and France in the 1860s, finally a match had been made.

"Invention breeds invention," according to Ralph Waldo Emerson. Soon Daimler's motorcycle turned into a true motorscooter with the engine plopped on a child's push toy rather than a bicycle. The French Auto-Fauteuil from 1902 and the Militaire from Cleveland, Ohio, from the 1910s used the step-through scooter design, avoiding the bulky gas tank between the legs and improving stability.

The Autoped of New York, looking less like a step-through motorcycle than a motorized child's toy, was the first scooter to be built in large numbers and available commercially around the country. In fact, after it was imported in 1916, "Autoped" became synonymous for "child's scooter" in Dutch. The Motoped set a new standard with a 1.5-horsepower engine mounted on the left side of the front wheel giving the scooter an awkward lean, later adopted by Piaggio's Vespa. The brakes relied on the magic of shoe leather, Fred Flintstone-

style. In other words, the Motoped needed some improvements.

The Autoped "Wonder of the Motor Vehicle World" was copied around Europe—some licensed and others not—by companies like Krupp in Germany (with a larger 200-cc engine), U.K. Imperial Motor Industries, and CAS in Czechoslovakia with a 155-cc (56x63) engine. While bicycles were being banned on many city roads due to residents terrorized by speed, the 1914 Autoped was made for sidewalk use. Even so, ads claimed that the scooter could hit 60 km/h (in reality, more like 25km/h).

Soon copies of the Autoped were popping up across the United States and Europe, each with minor improvements to the original. Germany had its DKW Golem & Megola and England had its Wilkinson. The English Autoglider De Luxe appeared in 1919, created by Charles Ralph Townsend at Townsend Engineering Company of Birmingham with a 269-cc Villiers engine mounted on a 16-inch front wheel. The Model A was seatless like the Autoped, but the Model D added a cushioned seat which doubled as suspension. Even though ads claimed top speed was 50

When Cushman began distributing Vespas—rather than its homespun Eagles, the Nebraska-based company added its own logo under the famous Vespa insignia.

*"It is a vehicle which, unlike the traditional motorcycle proper, is suitable for all social classes and for both sexes...It is the ideal vehicle for short trips to town for businessmen, professionals, doctors, etc."*
—Motociclismo, in a rare promotion of scooters, April 10, 1946

Cushman of Nebraska built motors and threw its hat in the scooter ring when it built a metal frame with wheels to accompany its motor. Then the Italians invaded with their Vespas and Lambrettas distributed through Sears, Roebuck and Montgomery Wards respectively. Cushman competed with the Italian upstarts, but eventually just distributed Vespas instead. Gloves and helmets are essential accessories to riding and protecting against unseemly road rash or irritating cracked skulls.

km/h, bold scooterists claimed to have reached 80 km/h, although probably on a steep incline.

## SALSBURY AND THE FIVE COMMANDMENTS OF SCOOTERS

The Salsbury Motor Glide was born in the back of a heating and plumbing shop in Oakland, California. E. Foster Salsbury had been inspired when he saw Amelia Earhart buzzing around on a Motoped in Burbank. "It got me started thinking about building a real scooter," recalled E. Foster Salsbury in 1992.

It was often pilots who kept the putt-putts alive from the first scooter wave since they were ideal for zipping down the tarmac to their planes. "Even the fast-flying airplane has to rely on the lowly scooter when taxiing into a parking area at the airport," wrote *Popular Mechanics* in 1947. After Salsbury and engineer Austin Elmore pieced together the first Motor Glide in 1936, famous aviator Colonel Roscoe Turner caught a whiff and was hooked. Soon Turner pushed Salsbury scooters whenever he went on the road with his airshow, and proclaimed, "The Salsbury Motor Glide is the greatest woman catcher I

have ever seen." Soon, even the likes of Bing Crosby dropped cash for a Motor Glide to pick up chicks.

While the 1936 Motor Glide wasn't much to look at, scribbled on the back of an early promotional photo from the Salsbury archives was written, "It worked fine on dry pavement." Nevertheless, its technological design revolutionized the scooter industry and was followed by all later scooters.

The 1937 Salsbury Motor Glide was further improved and so were the brochures, "Dash hither and yon in gay abandon...eases through traffic like an eel...." "It's as safe as an armchair and as comfortable..." The California-based company was worried about its image with the jet set and proclaimed its scooter "...an instant hit in the Hollywood movie colony...at swanky Palm Springs and gay Florida resorts." Even so, the groundbreaking scooter lacked the style that would be added a decade later, although it did offer a special seat "padded with felt and hair."

In 1938, updates included a revolutionary self-shifting transmission later copied by every scooter manufacturer from

Honda to Piaggio. The idea was simple—as the speed of the engine increased, the driver pulley was pushed together giving a bigger circumference for the belt to ride on and thereby increasing the "gear ratio." Salsbury again changed engine manufacturers—this time to Lauson motors, following previous trials with Evinrude and Johnson, and even a rejected bid for 1,000 Cushman Husky engines.

Meanwhile across town, Salsbury's Motor Glide had spawned competition when Albert G. Crocker received a call from motorcycle mogul Floyd Clymer of Los Angeles to help him hop on the scooter bandwagon. Thus, the Crocker Scootabout was born in the 1930s, adding beautiful Art Deco styling and a two-tone paint scheme—years before the Mods—to otherwise utilitarian-looking two-wheelers of which fewer than 100 were built. Salsbury had the jump on the competition.

To try and extend Salsbury scooter sales into Europe in 1938, an agent headed into the Old Country armed with blueprints and brochures to try and convince foreign manufacturers to sign on the dotted line. E. Foster Salsbury believed that one of the companies was Piaggio. Who knows what would have happened if the Vespa had never been conceived and Italy was motorized with Salsburys? Instead, ol' Benito and Adolf spoiled everything.

During World War II, Salsbury pitched into the war effort and worked on experimental wind tunnels to test out airplanes. No wonder the Salsbury Super-Scooter Model 85 was the most aerodynamic scooter ever made when it came out in 1946. In 1944–1945, Avion Inc., an L.A. war-material company, bought out Salsbury and based the company in Pomona, California. Northrup Aircraft Company later bought out Avion. Even so, they kept their loyalty to two-strokes and produced the sleekest scooter ever built, the Model 85. Engineer Lewis Thostenson was able to scrounge enough time during the war years to envision a Buck Rogers two-wheeler that would hit the showrooms just one year after the war.

Finally, Salsbury scooters veered from the name "Motor Glide"—easily confused with Cushman's ubiquitous "Auto Glide"—to just Salsbury. All the technological stops were pulled out as the new Super-Scooter was deemed the "MOST COMPLETELY AUTOMATIC VEHICLE EVER BUILT" by Salsbury ad copy. This two-wheeled marvel featured a special "Straight-Shot" carburetor, torque converter, one-sided front forks (similar to those on airplanes), and, of course, the automatic drive with fancy new words replacing the clumsy "brake and throttle" with the simpler "stop and go." Unfortunately, the Salsbury Super-Scooter only survived from 1946 to 1949, at which time it was run off the road by the huge

## SCOOTER STARS
### E. FOSTER SALSBURY:
### WHAT MAKES A SCOOTER A SCOOTER?

Apart from developing the sleekest scooters ever built and possibly inspiring Piaggio to build its Vespa, E. Foster Salsbury established the Five Commandments of Scooters, thanks to his 1936 Motor Glide. To be considered a scooter, the little two-wheeler must carry at least three of these traits:

1. Motor is placed under the rider, usually just in front of the rear wheel.
2. The chassis is step-through with no pesky bar between the rider's legs, and usually accompanied by a floorboard.
3. It has a covered motor and leg shield, to protect the rider from the elements and to hide the sloppy engine.

4. It has small wheels to increase maneuver ability—critics call it "tippy."
5. It has automatic transmission or a clutch, and gears are controlled by hand levers.

"Own it! Maintain it! Operate it!" shouted ad copy from an old *Popular Mechanics* from 1949 about the coveted Model 52. This classic Cushman was updated in 1950 as the Model 62 "family scooter" with a disastrous Variamatic torque converter that was constantly updated and "almost ruined the Cushman reputation for reliability," according to *A History of Cushman Motor Works.* Simple but effective summed up these early Cushman scooters, and the ads didn't deny it, "You just turn the throttle on the right hand handlebar to go, and step on the brake pedal to stop."

American cars of the 1950s.

## POWELL'S PUTT-PUTTS

During the depths of the Depression, designers saw the simplicity of Salsbury's Motor Glide. Entrepreneurs like the Powell brothers Channing and Hayward from Los Angeles pulled their tools out of retirement and reinvented the scooter wheel. The 2.3-horsepower Lauson engine with a centrifugal clutch could barely push the early Streamliner 40 up to 30 miles per hour. In 1940, Powell turned from mini-scooters to mini-motorcycles with the punning A-V-8 (Aviate), now a 5-horsepower engine with options like the first push-button start on a scooter.

Frank Cooper bought some A-V-8s, tattooed his own name on the gas tank, welded a web of metal to the frame, and submitted the "Cooper War Combat Motor Scooter" to the U.S. Army as a parachuting scooter. While Cooper's scooter impressed the doughboys, his makeshift factory left something to be desired, and the contract went to Nebraska's Cushman. Powell's remaining stock was bought out by Clark Engineering in 1942 and re-released as the Victory Clipper, and later as the Clark Cyclone.

By 1945, Powell could stop making rockets and shells, and fell back into the scooter biz with the Lynx. "Dreams do come true!" announced their flyers for the 6-horsepower putt-putt. The P-48 and P-49 models followed in 1948 and 1949 with the odd ad pitch, "It Looks Custom Built," meaning the unusual reinforcing crossbars welded in every direction were

### Personal Transportation News

For Business or Pleasure

For Men and Women

EVERYWHERE IN THE U. S.

# NEW SELF-SHIFTING MOTOR GLIDE HERE

*Powered like a truck! But it makes over a hundred miles on a Gallon. A 200 pound driver can go 30 miles per hour on it!*

**AUTOMATIC TRANSMISSION—AUTOMATIC CLUTCH**

*Nationally Recognized as one of the Automotive Industry's Outstanding Engineering Achievements of Recent Years.*

The heavy, rugged engine of the 1938 Salsbury Motor Glide assures its owner more power than he'll ever need. Motor rated 1 H.P. . . . develops 2 H.P. The most Remarkable Power Plant ever put into a Single-Passenger Vehicle. Ample power for speedy acceleration, for quick get-away in traffic. Ample power that *takes any hill* in stride! Finger-tip control! Automotive type float-feed carburetor with high and low speed mixture control. Here are some of its exclusive features:

1 **AUTOMATIC TRANSMISSION:** Shifts speeds *automatically*; no pedal or gear lever to work. Transmission ratio automatically varies from 14:1 in low to 4:1 in high according to road speed. The steeper the hill, the more power you get.

2 **AUTOMATIC CLUTCH:** Permits engine to idle when *Motor Glide* is standing. As throttle is opened, clutch automatically engages and you smoothly glide away.

3 **AUTOMATIC STARTING:** Engine starts easily with just a push of the Motor Glide—*No kicking or cranking.*

4 **BIGGER, SAFER BRAKE:** Positive safe-action, self-energizing type. Stops in 25 feet at 25 miles per hour.

**RIDE THIS SENSATIONAL NEW VEHICLE FOR THE GREATEST SURPRISE OF YOUR LIFE!**

**U. S. Mail Delivered by Motor Glide**

Care U. S. Post Office,
Chula Vista, California,
March 22, 1938.

Salsbury Corporation.

Gentlemen:

I am a letter carrier at the Post Office in this town and use one of your MOTOR GLIDES in my work.

I average 25 miles per day and stop and start from three to four hundred times a day. Have been doing this daily for nine months and the machine has stood up remarkably well but it now needs new rings.

I do not know their cost but can you send them C.O.D. as quickly as possible or advise me so the machine will not be laid up.

Thanking you, I am,

Sincerely,
H. L. BERGER.

**Travels 1300 Miles Using Only 12 Gallons of Gas**

Brownsville, Texas.
August 12, 1937.

Salsbury Corporation.

Gentlemen:

I am the guy that made the trip from Brownsville to Dallas about six hundred miles wide open all the way in about three days.

The machine stood the trip mighty well, in addition to my weight of a hundred and sixty pounds I carried a complete change of Khaki, tool kit, one quart of oil, one gallon of gasoline, a spare tire and tube and a rain coat. I used twelve gallons of gasoline and two quarts of oil round trip of about thirteen hundred miles of running.

I will go on record as saying that the Motor Glide is about the most practical thing of its kind that I have ever seen and it will do much better than you saw it will do. It is safe, for the reason that twelve of them have been in operation here for about six months, and no one has been hurt.

You will pardon the poor letter, the variation in stationery, and the typographical errors, I hope, I am not a stenographer, but I am a mechanic.

Respectfully yours,
(Signed) N. G. MARTIN,
Pan American Airways, Inc.,
Brownsville, Texas.

*Colonel Roscoe Turner on his 1938 Motor Glide*

"I rode the original MOTOR GLIDE in 1936 and I have been a MOTOR GLIDE enthusiast ever since, but the new 1938 MOTOR GLIDE with automatic transmission and automatic clutch is the last word in personal transportation and far exceeds my fondest expectation for performance."

**COL. ROSCOE TURNER.**

**WHY USE A CANNON** WHEN ALL YOU NEED IS A RIFLE ? AND WHY USE YOUR AUTOMOBILE WHEN ALL YOU NEED IS PERSONAL TRANSPORTATION ?

**SALSBURY CORPORATION** *MOTOR GLIDE* **INGLEWOOD, CALIFORNIA**

TRADE MARK REGISTERED

Printed in U. S. A.

---

*Powered Like a Truck!*
In late 1937, Salsbury introduced its most revolutionary invention ever: the "Self-Shifting Motor," as the firm termed its new automatic clutch and transmission torque converters on this poster hung in Salsbury dealer showrooms across the United States. And Roscoe Turner was back, as happy as ever, with his new 1938 Model 60 Motor Glide with 1½-horsepower Johnson engine. This automatic transmission technology was futuristic for 1937 and copied in some form even today.
*E. Foster Salsbury archives*

---

anything but streamlined.

Once the Korean War broke out, Powell was back to bombs, but soon returned to the transportation arena in 1954 by taking an old 1940s chassis off of a Plymouth and producing the ultimate camper with a trunk designed for fishing rods, pop-top camper, and wood bumpers. Taking mass-produced car accessories and putting them to new uses wasn't a stretch for Powell. After all, the A-V-8's ad pitch

threatened that it used "replacement parts of a popular low-priced automobile." In 1967, Powell rediscovered its roots in scooterdom, however, with the Model L & M Challenger and Phantom mini-bikes with Tecumseh Briggs & Stratton engines.

## MIDWESTERN MOTORSCOOTERS

Florence during the Renaissance, Paris in the 1920s, and the Midwest in the 1930s and 1940s were the places to be. Budding

The front headlamp of this Lambretta LD was mounted low on the legshield. This Innocenti scooter envolved, placing the headlight on the handlebars to move with the wheels.

entrepreneurs began piecing together scooters with any available metal they could rustle up, then selling them to trusting family and friends.

The Chicago-based Rock-Ola delved into the scooter world as a detour from the jukebox biz and "true weight" scales. The Rock-Ola Deluxe model was "powered with the proven Johnson 1-horsepower engine," which it glorified as the "Iron Horse"—perhaps "iron goat" would have been more appropriate.

Further north, in chilly Minneapolis, Comet Manufacturing tested the scooter waters by releasing a brochure featuring a Comet scooter that never went into production, according to a former mechanic. Of the Comets that actually did cruise down the bumpy backroads of Minnesota, *Popular Science* wrote that the marvelous suspension was "frame and seat," avoiding the luxury of springs to protect the rider's gluteus maximus.

Midget Motors of Kearney, Nebraska, went one better, offering pure luxury on its 1938 Puddlejumper with "any model available with parcel carriers, windshield for dust, rain, snow, or winter operation, and even a powerful radio!" The scooter's streamlined styling and optional gas or electric engines were eons ahead of their time; one of the Puddlejumper models was "self-balancing" through the simple miracle of having three wheels.

Postwar, Gambles five-and-dime stores wanted to delve into the scooter battle against Montgomery Ward and Sears, Roebuck and Company with the peewee putt-putt called the Doodlebug, manufactured by Beam of Webster City, Iowa. The name Doodlebug was already synonymous for scooters throughout the United States, only this time it was copyrighted. In pre-Doodlebug days, *Time* magazine wrote in a 1939 article about "Postman Smith" who "stands at the back of his doodlebug, putt-putting along at four to twelve miles an hour. For a delivery, he leaves his scooter contentedly burbling at the curb, manages to save not only foot-power but some 23 percent of the time formerly needed to cover his route."

A common theme of Vespa club stickers is the wasp (or *vespa* in Italian) with an encircling gear, which dates back to clubs' original founding in the 1950s.

Nearly every motorcycle maker had made a swipe at the scooter market, so in 1960 Harley-Davidson decided to throw its hat into the ring. While most scooters borrowed ideas from fighter planes, café racers, helicopters, or Ferraris, the Wisconsin wonder's Topper seemed to borrow the concept of a bass boat. The fiberglass body and pull-start cord seemed like the perfect scooter for hauling in a northern pike. Being the little brother to world famous motorcycles, the Harley Topper could never live up to that rebel image, even with Kookie from *77 Sunset Strip* pushing the putt-putts with ad copy like, "Kookie, where's your Topper?"

In the lengthy definitive history, *Harley-Davidson: The Milwaukee Marvel*, the Topper is allotted one sentence. Most

*"Dash hither and yon in gay abandon...eases through traffic like an eel...It's as safe as an armchair and as comfortable..."*
—*1937 Salsbury Motor Glide ad*

books on the company regard the misunderstood scooter as a mistake better left to gather dust in the garage. Trying to get back to its old image, Harley ads in the 1970s showed a group of Hell's Angels and the text asked if you would sell an inferior product to these guys—unless, of course, it was a Topper.

### NORMAN SIEGAL OF MOTO SCOOT
"The Henry Ford of the scooter business."
—*Time 4/3/39*

Norman "Abe" Siegal's legs ached and he was sick of dropping two bits to take the streetcar across Chicago in 1934. While Al Capone was busy bullet-proofing his limousine with steel, Siegal removed an engine from a gasoline-powered washing machine. "He used two wheels from my baby buggy," recalls his son Burt. "He rigged it up so he could hook it to the rear bumper of the car. People saw him riding it during the depths of the Depression and asked him to make one for them." Although zoot-suited gang-

White walls are back! For years, getting scooter-sized white wall tires was next to impossible, so purists tried to revamp old, worn out white walls for that classic—if dangerous—look.

The left sidepanel of the Vespa has gone through various, and sometimes bizarre, transformations. The glovebox in this photo may seem like a good idea, but the whole design of the Vespa carries the engine (and the heaviest part of the scooter) on the right side. Best put a brick in your glovebox to balance the weight.

sters probably scoffed at this makeshift contraption, Siegal's invention made him a millionaire while Al was doing time for a slight tax problem.

Norm soon rented a Chicago storefront, promising to pay rent as soon as he sold his first batch of ten scooters. Using his old-fashioned American ingenuity when he ran out of metal, "he broke a hole in the wall of his store, and pulled out a lead water pipe," recalls Burt Siegal. Thus the very first Moto Scoots were born. "When he got paid, he just replaced the pipe."

In 1936, when Norm was only 24 years old, he officially set up shop in part of a west-side Chicago factory. "By the end of the year he had sold 186 of them at $109 apiece and had taken over the whole factory. In 1937 the output was 2,700," according to a 1939 *Time* article.

Surpassing retail sales of $500,000 in 1938, Moto Scoot moved to 8440 South Chicago Ave. where they had a banked gravel race track running around the building so employees could let off steam by taking a couple of laps around the building. (The winged Moto Scoot logo graced the marquee in the now run-down factory until

1996.) In a 1938 *Chicago Daily Times* article, Siegal was surely misquoted as saying that he "…recommends it for the gent too indolent to walk to work and too antisocial to ride a street car."

Since Siegal had been on the county fair dirt track circuit racing "Fronty-Fords" before he pounded out his first puddle-jumper, he souped up a three-wheeled racing Moto Scoot and rented it to tourists at Navy Pier to let them feel the power of a two-stroke. He also worked on a two-seater "quarter-in-the-slot" rentable scooter to zoom gawkers around the futuristic 1939 World's Fair.

Still having racing fever from his "Fronty-Ford" days, Siegal built a half-sized racing Moto Scoot with a two-cycle Villiers engine and four-speed transmission that so aptly put the competition to shame with its speed and maneuverability that it was banned from motorcycle races. To celebrate his success in sales and racing, Siegal built a gold-plated Moto Scoot in 1941. The tide was turning against him, though, when hard times hit home. In 1941, Siegal signed a chattel mortgage on his patents and machinery to make payroll. He ended up

**On the early scooters (in this case a Lambretta LD), the gas and two-stroke oil must be mixed together in the same tank. In Italy, mixed leaded gas and oil, or *miscela*, was available at every gas station. Nowadays to avoid having a pesky engine seize, scooterists with classics must carefully measure each liquid then shake the scooter for maximum mixing.**

losing the Moto Scoot dies to American Moto Scoot, which didn't begin scooter production again until 1945. Even so, Siegal's vision of getting off the tram and onto a putt-putt was confirmed by *Popular Mechanics* in 1947, "[A scooter'] low cost of operation means it can be used for commuting to work daily at about the same expense as streetcar riding."

## "CUSHMAN": AMERICAN SYNONYM FOR SCOOTER

Cushman Motor Works of Omaha, Nebraska, entered the scooter world by happenstance. No staff of highly trained engineers envisioned America's future being brought together coast-to-coast on Cushman two-wheelers.

It began in 1913 by the Cushman family building the hearty Husky engine to power the likes of its Bob-a-Lawn mowers. The Depression hit hard, and in 1934 fellow Nebraska natives, the Ammons, bought out the Cushman plant. The Ammons envisioned this newly acquired factory as just an engine production line, but that would all change when a young neighbor boy zoomed by in a pieced-together, rough-and-ready scooter.

The story began when aviator Colonel Roscoe Turner came to Nebraska with his daredevil airshow in 1936. As a spokesman for Salsbury Motor Glides, part of Roscoe Turner's spectacle featured pilots driving to their planes on these barn-storming little putt-putts. "A neighborhood kid saw this scooter and decided that it would be fun to have one of his own. He found some angle iron and wheelbarrow wheels and built himself a motorscooter. And he used a Cushman 'Husky' engine from a lawn mower to power it," according to Cushman president Robert Ammon in a 1995 interview.

When "Uncle Charlie" Ammon noticed the boy buying spare parts for his homemade gadabout, a lightbulb appeared over his head and the Auto-Glide was born. "The frame was made from one-and-a-quarter-inch angle iron, but we soon learned that it wasn't enough. We then used two-inch channel iron, which did the job," recalls Bob Ammon. Of course this was the age before product liability laws, so if a

While the Vespa kept its engine on the right side due to its monocoque construction, the Lambretta's tubular construction allowed it to be centered and more balanced. Both side panels on the Lambretta gave access to different parts of the engine, magneto, carburetor, and rear brakes.

scooter collapsed under the driver's hefty load they just brought it back. "When I got the scooter stable enough that I could drive it without hands, I knew it was ready." This little prototype ran on a couple of 4x8-inch wheelbarrow tires and a borrowed Husky engine from a Bob-A-Lawn mower.

The Auto-Glide was an afterthought to Cushman. "The idea of making a motorscooter was to build and sell more engines," according to Robert Ammon. In fact, early Auto-Glides were crude machines with no suspension, just balloon tires and a padded seat. Even so, a 1937 Cushman letter to potential buyers proclaimed the Auto-Glide "the very latest genuine AMERICAN THRILL." A brochure from the same year made the bizarre claim that driving an Auto-Glide was actually "NO COST AT ALL. Why, it's actually cheaper than walking." Apparently truth in advertising was not par for the course.

The key to the scooter biz is to keep an eye on the competition and don't let vanity get in the way of making enhancements. To improve on the original design, Robert Ammon recalled, "I saw other scooters—Moto-Scoot, Salsbury, Powell, and others. We would buy them to look them over to

see what good features they had that we could incorporate. We also had lots of suggestions from dealers and employees within the company." Each year the Auto-Glide was refined, at least until the dawns of World War I and World War II.

During the war years, since scooters were considered an economical form of civilian transportation, Robert Ammon remembered, "We were making scooters when Ford couldn't get tires to make cars." The Cushman Model 53 was more than just a way to burn rationed gas, and the 82nd and 101st Airborne decided that it was just the ticket to liberate Europe. Perhaps secret documents were leaked to the United States about Mussolini's Volugrafo paratrooper scooter, or confidential blueprints were shared with the British about the RAF's Corgi Welbike. Whatever the reason, the U.S. Army Air Force decided they needed a secret scooter weapon.

On April 29, 1943, Cushman responded to bids from the War Department for an attack scooter. However, Cooper Motors of Los Angeles was also one of the finalists, with its 5-horsepower Cooper War Combat Motor Scooter debuting on February 17, 1944 in Detroit, according to

**Just like Scarface wore his wound with pride, so must scooterists wear the dings and scratches on their Vespas. At least they've survived to tell the tale and haven't given up on their ride.**

*"Cushman scooters have all the soup the average American will ever need."*
—Mechanix Illustrated, *1956*

From a distance, this scooter looks like a Vespa. In fact, the Indian company Bajaj was set up by Piaggio—after the Indian CEO was blessed by none other than Mahatma Ghandi. Just as the English colonialists were tired of drinking gin and tonics and set India free, so did the Italians at Piaggio. Now, Bajaj is free to make Vespa clones—called Chetak—till the holy cows come home.

secret "Characteristic Sheets" on various models tested. When army bureaucrats weren't satisfied with their visit to the Cooper factory, they turned around and gave the contract to Cushman. Cushman engineers got busy reinforcing the airborne scooter to be dropped from the heavens deep into

enemy territory. They pitched a rope over a tree branch, tied it to the Cushman, lugged it into the air, then let go and sent the scooter crashing to the earth. When the Model 53 had enough reinforcement to not fall apart, it was ready for the putt-putt Blitzkrieg.

When Cushman returned to civilian

*"Cheaper Than Shoe Leather!"*
**With such relatively great gas mileage on early scooters, Cushman touted its putt-putts as actually cheaper than walking. No wonder Gulf penny-pinched by using a scooter for delivery on the tarmac.**

life after the war, the Auto-Glide name was dropped, opting for the now established "Cushman" title and calling the new line of the 52, 52A, and 54 "The Family Scooter." Updates included an automatic clutch on the 54 model, and the long-awaited suspension to give that "F-L-O-A-T-I-N-G sensation"––at least until you hit a pothole.

Rather than resting on its laurels, Cushman brought Alfred Sloan of GM's idea of "planned obsolescence" to the scooter world with annual technological updates so fashionable folks would only want the latest model. "Most people think that obsolescence means the end. It means

the beginning. People always live with obsolescent attitudes and in obsolescent frames of mind and obsolescent technologies and homes," said cultural icon Marshall McLuhan. With heady ideas like this in mind, the Ammons brought out a dazzling array of models while other companies tended to just rehash the same old ideas.

Prewar ad pitches like "Cheaper than shoe leather" and "Sell more ice cream" were a thing of the past. An old 1939 ad that boasted, "You can glide for 1/3 cent per mile!" tripled to "1 cent per mile" by 1949. (Inflation or gas guzzler?) The quantity of oil a Cushman burned was promptly

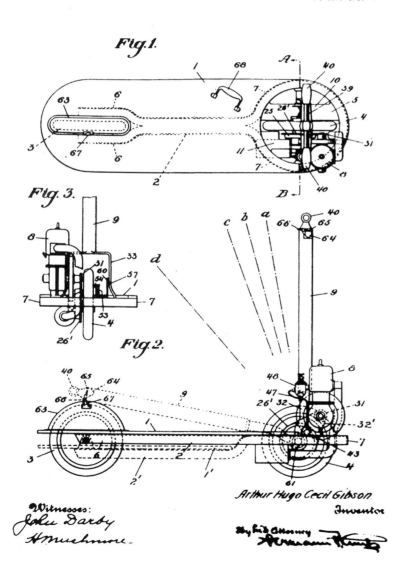

A. H. C. GIBSON.
SELF PROPELLED VEHICLE.
APPLICATION FILED JULY 24, 1913. RENEWED SEPT. 28, 1915.
1,192,514. Patented July 25, 1916.

*Autoped Patent*

**Scooter historians have debated whether the first scooter was French, Danish, or English, but the American Autoped ranks among the earliest as proven by this patent filed in 1913 and approved in 1916. Nearly one hundred years later, a new mini scooter revival would copy this early Autoped design and ignore any modern improvements made in the past century. History repeats as 10,000 injuries in 2004 were attributed to these new skateboard-like motorized scooters with miniscule wheels that make the ingenious Autoped of 1916 look absolutely modern.**

**Skootamota**
Created by English engineer Granville Bradshaw with a hefty 147cc intake-over-exhaust motor, the Skootamota was marketed as the perfect mobile for ladies since the floorboard allowed the latest dresses or risqué swimsuits to be worn without that bothersome bar between the legs. *François-Marie Dumas*

*"I'm profoundly convinced that the history and successes of Piaggio—along with its failures and less happy times— are intimately tied to Italian exuberance that is part of our genetic makeup."*
—*Giovanni Agnelli, owner of Fiat and Piaggio*

If you want to portray more of a bad boy (or girl) image aboard your scooter, try screwing spikes onto your helmet.

deleted from print ads. Perhaps consumers finally realized that the 1937 Cushman ad for "500 Miles on a Quart of Oil!" simply meant having to rebuild the engine every 1,000 miles. Through constant advertising in *Popular Mechanics*, Cushman threw out the window historian John Kenneth Galbraith's claim that "Few people at the beginning of the nineteenth century needed an ad man to tell them what they wanted."

Cushman continued pulling its weight in postwar reparations as part of the European Recovery Act. Belgian Cushman was established in 1950 in Anderlues, Belgium, building bizarre off-shoots of the American scooters complete with Husky engines, Cushman chassis, and imaginative (and never copied) styling. Even a three-wheeled delivery mobile was offered for "business, factories, Sunday drives, and sports."

Finally, by the early 1950s Cushman hit its stride with the Pacemaker and the early RoadKing scooters. Robert Ammon remembered unabashedly, "We got some ideas from Vespa and Lambretta," just as Piaggio and Innocenti had originally gotten inspiration from Cushman. The result of these new models established the name "Cushman" as synonymous with "scooter" in the United States.

With the tenacity of an entrepreneur, Cushman threw Salsbury's Five Commandments of Scooters out the

window and bred a Harley Hog with a Doodlebug to produce the staple of the Cushman line: the Eagle. "Somebody in our sales department wanted a scooter that looked like a motorcycle with the gas tank between your legs. It turned out to be a hell of a good idea," said Robert Ammon.

Spurred by demand for a cheap "second car," the Eagle offered just the ticket, and with rumors of the Korean War in the 1950s, *Business Week* pronounced, "War talk has brought a sellers' market in automobiles, it has also started a boom in the motorscooter field." In that year, Cushman Motor Works expected to produce 10,000 scooters with $3.5 million in sales.

Every couple of years, dramatic improvements came to the Eagle—a far cry from the pokey Auto-Glides of the 1930s. From the Super Eagle to the Silver Eagle, Cushman updated their models with electric starters, better suspension, and larger engines. *Mechanix Illustrated* pronounced in 1956 that "Cushman scooters have all the soup the average American will ever need."

*Popular Science* raved in 1957 of the Cushman RoadKing's "Detroit Styling" because of its sporty two-tone paint, and "Thanks to an automatic clutch, the Cushman is the simplest to drive. Twist the throttle open, and you're off to a silk-smooth start every time. To stop, simply step on the brake." By 1957, 650 dealers across

the United States were proudly displaying the latest models in their storefronts.

The next year, the consequences of the youth market hopping on scooters was finally felt. In the 1950s, legislation was passed raising the minimum age of scooterists, but even so, teenagers were being killed in scooter accidents by scores. In Ohio alone, scooter mishaps resulted in 11 deaths and 412 injuries. An industry shill went on the offensive and declared that bicycles were responsible for twice as many deaths as these innocent putt-putts. Cushman put out comic books consisting of part advertising, part safety guide, for teenagers. *Business Week* praised their efforts in February 1959: "Cushman, while against legislation now pending, holds that dealers should make sure their customers have proper training. To this end, it has set up safety classes in several states."

The final nail in Cushman's scooter coffin wasn't safety, however, but competition from overseas. Rather than bow out, Cushman decided to distribute Vespas themselves beginning in 1961, attaching their own logo to the legshield as the new Cushman scooter. Many shocked dealers refused to give in to the competition, and

instead opted to sell Hondas. Robert Ammon conceded that "The Hondas were just frankly better machines than the Cushman Eagles—and they were cheaper."

## ITALIAN DESIGN CONQUERS THE WORLD

The "Second Italian Renaissance" flourished in Italy following World War II as the age of mass mobilization hit even the smallest Italian hill town. In 1946, rubble was all that was left of the wartime factories, but the seed of knowledge to mass-produce machines had already been sown.

The Italian Futurists' idea that "War is the world's only hygiene" had been thoroughly debunked, but their other axiom of "the religion of speed" still rang true. Italian engineers began producing fine-tuned motorcycles and scooters with Marinetti's famous quote ringing in their heads, "Time and space died yesterday," meaning all that was left was speed. The famous Futurist went on to write, "We say that the world's magnificence has been enriched by a new beauty: the beauty of speed."

The Vespa's parent company, Piaggio, can trace its roots to Rinaldo Piaggio's 1884 sawmill, which eventually made ships for

**Stopped at a red light, this vintage scooter club awaits two-by-two. On the move at high speeds, however, staggered riding allows more room to dodge around obstacles.**

*"Postman Smith stands at the back of his doodlebug, putt-putting along at four to twelve miles an hour. For a delivery, he leaves his scooter contentedly burbling at the curb, manages to save not only foot-power but some 23 percent of the time formerly needed to cover his route."*
—Time *magazine, 1939, advocating scooter use for mailmen in pre-Doodlebug times.*

*Salsbury Model 85 DeLuxe*
**Towards the end of WWII, Lewis Thostenson designed the ultimate spaceship-cum-scooter, the coveted Model 85. Debuting in 1946, the age of the children's motorized putt-putt was over and instead 700 to 1,000 Jet Age Salsburys hit the streets of L.A. The Model 85 came in two forms with the same 6-horsepower engines: the Standard and the DeLuxe with added Plexiglas fairing. In spite of its blast-off design, the Model 85 is a cinch to maneuver, "There's no clutch lever, no gear shift...*Stop* and *Go* pedals are the only controls."** *E. Foster Salsbury archives*

the navy. During World War I, Piaggio set up shop near Pisa, and became famous for its sturdy airplanes and the first air-cooled airplane engine in 1924. Building two- to four-engine planes during World War II, the Piaggio factory was a natural target to be flattened by B1 bombers.

Rising from the wreckage, Rinaldo Piaggio's sons Enrico and Armando kept the spirit alive by producing the Vespa, "the most important of all new Italian design phenomena," according to *Design* magazine in 1949.

The postwar saga began in February, 1945 when designer Corradino D'Ascanio made a few sketches of a little prototype scooter. Called the MP6 with a unique monocoque body and attractive shielding of the engine, it had just a small problem of an overheating engine. Having originally been a helicopter designer, D'Ascanio easily worked out the flaws and his perfected scooter— named the Vespa—went on to mobilize the Italian masses. More than 50 years later, D'Ascanio can take his place next to Ghia, Farina of Pininfarina, Ponti, and DaVinci, since the Vespa appeared as a tribute to Italian design in the Guggenheim museum next to a classic Olivetti typewriter.

Enrico Piaggio tooted his own horn in a 1956 *Time* interview, "Just like Henry Ford put the workers on wheels in America, we put automotive transport within the

reach of people who never expected to travel that way." That same year, *Newsweek* reported that "1.5 million scooters were on the roads in Italy."

Now remote little villages that rarely saw outsiders had buzzing Vespas braving the cobblestones of the town piazza. *American Mercury* reported in 1957 that "Wherever donkeys go, the Vespa goes too."

As soon as Vespas were poised to cross the Atlantic, American magazines took a different attitude. Vespas were condescendingly called Italians' "little machines" by *Business Week* in 1956, and were said to be driven carelessly thanks to Italians' "Latin enthusiasm."

The *New Yorker* feared the two-stroke fury zooming down Broadway and warned in 1956, "Motor scooters, the current scourge of sleep in Italian cities, have established a beachhead here."

In Italy, however, the Piaggio brothers were heroes because they put Italy on wheels. By the time the 1950s and 1960s rolled around, with political turmoil threatening the Italian state, the majority Communist party was kept from power due to the C.I.A. and the Vespa. Enrico Piaggio deemed it his patriotic duty to put his putt-putts within reach of the workers to lure them away from Gramsci and Marx. "The best way to fight Communism in this country is to give each worker a scooter, so he will have his own transportation, have something valuable of his own, and have a stake in the principle of private property," Piaggio told *Time* in 1952.

Therefore, owning a Vespa was an Italian's patriotic duty. "Roaring, darting scooters, outnumbering automobiles, dominate Rome's traffic. These toylike vehicles have swept Italy since the war, almost replacing the motorcycle," according to a 1957 *National Geographic* article.

## JAPAN: THE LAND OF THE RISING SCOOTER

While Europe and America were concentrating on style, Japan was busy making the most practical and reliable scooters the world had ever seen. The Fuji Rabbit was the first on the scene in 1946, matching Piaggio's timetable on the other side of the globe, and borrowing heavily from the 1930s American scooter revolution. While only eight Fujis were born with the 135-cc four-stroke engine that year, the Rabbits multiplied and morphed into slick steeds in the 1950s with a curved design, long wheelbase, and peppy, 125-cc engines. The luxury line of the Fuji S-61 and the Superflow followed Honda's footsteps in the 1960s as Fuji tried to keep up with Honda's ubiquitous Cub moped.

Another Japanese giant, Mitsubishi, gave up production of its Zero-San fighter planes, seeing little future in the kamikaze market (not being allowed to build planes postwar), and wisely opted for the scooter field with its chunky-looking C-11 Pigeon. Within a few years, a designer's touch turned the Pigeon into the sleek Silver Pigeon, becoming one of the mainstays of the Japanese market. The Mitsubishi mark still reminded American vets of the Pacific arena, so when Rockford of Illinois imported Pigeons, they conveniently hid the Japanese emblem with their own. In the late 1950s, Montgomery Ward bought out Rockford, renaming them Riverside the

Pigeons tropical model names like Nassau, Miami, and Waikiki (Pearl Harbor didn't make the list).

The little putt-putt that could, however, was the Honda. Howing produced more mopeds/scooters than any other company in the world. As the son of a blacksmith, Soichiro Honda's talent ranged from piston rings to airplane propellers to motorized bicycles. 1947 saw the Model A moped built by 13 employees in a small 12x18-foot shed. In 1953, the Cub clip-on engine was born from this original design, becoming the Cub scooter, which proliferated around the world with more than 15 million built. In spite of the omnipresent mopeds/scooter wannabes, Honda produced space-age scooters with bizarre chrome airducts and styling perfect for any *Blade Runner* android. Beginning with the Juno KA in 1954, with a 189-cc overhead-valve engine, and the 1955 Juno KB with a 220-cc, 9-horsepower motor, the world wasn't ready for these glossy mounts, and waited for the mini putt-putts that Honda and Yamaha would later produce.

Another way to look tougher aboard your scooter is to give your scooter club a really nasty sounding name. No one is going to mess with a member of "The Defilers."

# BUYING THE RIGHT SCOOTER

## WHAT YOU WILL LEARN

- How to avoid buyer's remorse and owner's self-hatred
- The difference between sport, classic, and maxi scooters
- The difference between all those damn Vespa models
- What are the most popular scooters in the world today?
- Should you spring for a vintage or modern scooter?
- Shifting and braking so you don't crash on your first time out

**Mod Museum**
Somehow Reggie Williams' pristine Vespa only enhances the ultramodern Weisman Art Museum designed by crazy Canuck architect Frank Gehry. Who says Vespas aren't space age? Or as Vespa designer Corradino d'Ascanio boasted, "The Vespa will always look like it does, even when it is powered by a mini nuclear reactor or as a vehicle to drive on the moon."

We live in a new golden age of scooterdom, with choices to satisfy even the most finicky scooterist. The only problem is: which ride to choose? New or used? Automatic or manual? Which brand? Engine size? Paint scheme? Most of these choices are personal preferences that can only be realized once atop that bench seat with the throttle spun wide open, but some are more practical. Will you be riding on surface streets where the speeds seldom exceed 40 miles per hour? If so, you might find a 50-cc scooter satisfactory. If you find yourself riding on streets where speeds reach 50 to 60 miles per hour, you will need a scooter with a bit more scoot, perhaps something in the 125-cc to 200-cc range. If you intend to do any freeway riding where speeds can exceed 80 miles per hour, you will need something 200 cc or larger.

### BRAND-NEW SCOOTERS

More new scooters are available today than during the boom years of the 1950s and 1960s, when every motorcycle manufacturer wanted to get a piece of the pie. This won't be a complete buyer's guide, since the new scooter lineup is forever changing, but it will give you a general idea about what's available. Check the manufacturer websites and your local motorcycle and scooter shops for the very latest models.

Scooters fall into three main categories: classic, sport, and maxi. Retro classic scooters are inspired by the bulbous Streamline Moderne styling from the 1950s and 1960s. Sport scooters are tricked-out mini crotch rockets with sharp, angular lines that look like they're topping 60 miles per hour even when parked next to a Yugo. Maxi scooters may intimidate less-experienced riders because of their gargantuan size (sometimes topping 650-cc), but they are highly capable machines. They are able to transport their riders from coast to coast in unrivaled comfort—the larger twin-cylinder models can even handle a rider and a passenger on such a

trip—and they can leave any Rocker on a classic café racer eating their dust.

When kicking tires at the scooter shop, don't forget to test drive (if possible) and don't believe everything the salespeople say. Shop the competition and ask what they think of the scooter shop across town. The Internet also provides a handy way to peruse scooters. Included here are some manufacturer web addresses. One note about the web addresses listed below: Many of these manufacturers are located in Italy and, like many Italian companies, are often in varying stages of insolvency. Their websites may or may not be operational. Consider it part of the Italian scooter's charm.

## APRILIA

**www.apriliausa.com**
Aprilia's wildly successful Scarabeo scooter harkened back to the Moto Guzzi Galletto with its large diameter wheels. Named for the sacred Egyptian beetle, the Scarabeo was soon reproduced in larger sizes (Scarabeo 50 Street, 50, 100, 125, 250, and 500) and the swarms filled Italian *piazze*. The Mojito Custom 50 and 150 strived to draw from the old-time scooter days with a cross between a Lambretta and a panhead Harley.

Italian teenagers often don't care about any ho-hum nostalgia or the good ol' days, so Italjet and Aprilia released a line of rocket scooters that look more like a Ferrari Modena than a Piaggio Paperino. The SR 50 Ditech and Sportcity 125 or 200

satisfied this lust for speed and the latest fashion, at least for the moment. The Atlantic 200 even comes in an enormous maxi-scooter version with a 500-cc engine for cross-country touring rather than putzing to the dairy store.

Currently the importation of Aprilia scooters into the U. S. market is questionable. Piaggio owns Aprilia and the company has announced that it intends to focus on developing the Piaggio brand in the U. S. market for the time being.

## BAJAJ

**www.bajajusa.com**
Blessed by Mahatma Ghandi himself, Bajaj began importing Vespas to India in 1948. Soon Piaggio allowed Bajaj to manufacture its own scooters and break from the Italian yoke completely in 1972. Bajaj offered a long line of scooters and "autorickshaws," but the most widely exported was the Bajaj Chetak (essentially a Vespa in Indian armor). As a low-priced alternative to an authentic Piaggio Vespa, the Chetak kept the Vespa PX series styling with upgrades like a four-stroke engine, turn signals, anti-dive front suspension, and electric start.

The four-stroke engine is an appealing feature for many environmentally conscious scooterists. Traditionally scooters have used two-stroke engines because they generally produce more power from a given engine capacity. But they also produce far more pollutants. Two-strokes use a total-

**Unsheathed Lambretta**
While most Mods dream of getting their paws on a Lambretta Series II or Slimline, Italians itch to uncover one of the early "uncovered" or "unsheathed" Lambrettas in their grandfather's barn. This beauty is housed at Vittorio Tessera's scooter museum in Rodano outside of Milan.

loss oiling system; rather than maintaining lubricating oil in a separate reservoir as on a four-stroke, lubricating oil is mixed with the fuel, charged, and burned during the combustion process. This is what causes the smoky exhaust that characterizes two-stroke engines. It also gives the Environmental Protection Agency (EPA) sleepless nights.

Two-strokes will soon be historical artifacts, like casual sex and Ford's flathead V-8 auto engine, and that's probably a good thing from an environmental standpoint, but it does signify the end of the classic scooter––almost. The Bajaj Chetak looks for all of the world like a classic Vespa, yet its clean-burning four-stroke engine satisfies both the EPA's exhaust sniffers and environmentalists alike. If you want classic style without classic pollution levels, the Chetak is your scoot.

## BETA

### www.betamotor.com

Just as the Medici controlled Renaissance artists in Florence, so Beta tries to keep out the Pisan scourge from modern Florence. Beta has opted for the sport scooter line that appeals to testosterone-fueled Italian *ragazzi*. With dashing multi-colored neon bikes—the Ark and Eikon—Michael Schumacher would turn green. Apart from the larger 125 or 150 Eikon, all the scooters fall into the 50-cc category to allow Italian 14-year-olds to navigate between the Ferraris and Fiats on Italian streets.

## DERBI

### www.derbiusa.net

Derbi, an acronym for Derivados de Bicicletus ("or Derived from Bicycles"), began in Spain in 1953. In the new millennium, Derbi offers modern-looking two-wheelers for teenagers who love speed. The 49-cc Atlantis two-stroke comes as the City, Bullet, or Wave, with different paint schemes to match even the flashiest of tennis shoes.

## HONDA

### www.honda.com

Honda has kept alive its two now "classic" modern scooters: the Elite and the Helix. The little 80-cc Elite has an illustrious career stemming back to Devo and Adam Ant when MTV first hit the small screen. The Helix was the original Barcalounger-cum-UFO to hit the scooter world.

Around the same time the Vespa returned to the United States, Honda responded with its classy Metropolitan, as part of its new line of sport, maxi, and classic models. Although the 50-cc, four-stroke Metropolitan draws from the classic styling of early Italian models, the Metropolitan uses a plastic body for its two-tone covering. This automatic scooter even features a combined braking system, so when the scooterist clutches the left handlebar lever, both front and rear brakes stop the little two-wheeler. To appeal to a broad market, Honda offers edible-sounding paint schemes like kiwi, blue hibiscus, juice, and salsa.

At the same time, Honda is trying to broaden the scooter market with the Honda

Ruckus, a bizarre mix of two-wheeled ATV and mini-Humvee. The fat tires and camouflage design on this 49-cc scooter make it perfect for dragging dead deer out of the woods. (Honda's 250-cc Big Ruckus is for hauling moose.)

Honda's 582-cc Silver Wing is one of the most popular maxi scooters on the market. It's also one of the largest and most luxurious. With a two-cylinder four-stroke and fuel-injected engine, this beast is more like a 100-mile-per-hour sofa with ABS than a motorcycle. The Silver Wing is a remarkable machine, capable of transporting two super-sized adults across continents while maintaining a scooter's agility and fun factor. The big Wing is attracting converts from the motorcycle world as well as scooterists wanting to move up to a larger machine.

## ITALJET

**www.italjet.com**

Into the 1990s, Italjet offered three 49-cc plastic scooters for three different careers: the Shopping, Reporter, and Bazooka. The most revolutionary scooter of the early 1990s, however, was the Velocifero, one of the first scooters to re-adapt the classic rotund Vespa styling of the 1940s and 1950s. The success of this scooter put other marques on notice that much of the public didn't care for miniature sport bikes, but wanted a rehash of Corradino D'Ascanio's original vision.

In 2004, Italjet announced plans for another maxi-scooter, the Marcopolo, with a powerful 500-cc engine and automatic transmission traveling on 17-inch wheels. More shocking is the Italjet Scoop, a hybrid between a scooter and a three-wheeler. Two wheels on the front of the space pod make it

**Vespa handlebars and headstock have undergone countless minor updates since the classic clamshell speedos of the early wide-body scooters.**

**Not all vintage scooters are pampered garage queens, only brought out for rallies and *Quadrophenia* screenings. Some, like this battered Vespa, are daily drivers.**

To keep your scooter from being swiped, take out the ignition key and secure the column lock (located along the right side on this Vespa). Better yet, get a kryptonite and lock the whole shebang to a post. The old Vespa keys are easily picked.

## MAXI SCOOTERS

If you plan to ride your scooter on limited-access freeways, you will need a scooter capable of traveling at least 70 miles per hour, which is how fast freeway traffic moves in most metropolitan areas. Generally this means buying a larger-displacement scooter, often referred to as a "maxi scooter."

Suzuki's Burgman series, available in 400-cc and 650-cc versions, and Honda's 600-cc Silver Wing are some of the most popular scooters of this type, but there are smaller, more agile scooters that provide adequate performance for freeway use.

Perhaps the smallest scooter capable of traveling at this speed is Piaggio's BV200 (called the Beverly 200 in markets other than the U.S. market). While most 200-cc scooters would probably be insufficient for freeway use, the Beverly is Italian—which means that while the electrics are questionable, the little sucker can go, and is easily capable of hitting 75–80 miles per hour. The overachieving engine will humble most 250-cc engines propelling the Asian scooters. But before you take your Beverly out on the freeways, check the laws of your state. Some states ban vehicles with engines under a certain displacement and while the Beverly might be capable, it might not be legal.

Bringing your vintage, classic, or modern scooter to a rally is a great way to horse-trade for a new scooter or parts for your ride.

impossible to tip and give worried parents peace of mind when junior hits the road.

## KYMCO

**www.kymco.com**

Kymco is a major player in the world scooter market, and has been making tremendous gains in the U.S. market. With a line of scooters that ranges from hot-rod 50-cc two-strokes to 500-cc maxi scooters (and even a genuine motorcycle), it's easy to see why.

Kymco has one of the most complete lineups in the scooter world. Beginning with the basic bargain-priced ZX50, which features an air-cooled two-stroke engine, a Kymco customer can move up to a variety of other models. The liquid-cooled Super 9 is one of the fastest 50-cc scooters on the market. For these 49-cc oil-injected two-strokes, Kymco has kept the price within range of teenagers in search of speed.

The more classic lines are left for the People scooters that are reminiscent of Aprilia's Scarabeo, which is in turn a copy of Moto Guzzi's Galletto. The sporty Bet and Win models feature more modern styling than the retro People models, and the Grand Vista and Xciting have the touring market covered.

## DOES SIZE MATTER?

What's better: 10 inches or 16 inches? When it comes to the diameter of scooter wheels, there is no easy answer to that question because it depends on what kind of handling characteristics a scooter rider values. One thing is certain—wheel diameter makes a huge difference in the way a scooter handles.

Traditional scooters roll on small-diameter, skinny wheels. Modern retro-styled scooters replicate traditional wheel and tire sizes, none more faithfully than the Stella, which rolls on tiny, 10-inch-diameter, 3.5-inch-wide rims. At the other extreme are scooters like the Piaggio Beverly, Aprilia Scarabeo, and Kymco People series, all of which feature motorcycle-sized 16-inch rims. Other scooters split the difference. For example, the Vespa Gran Turismo rolls on 12-inch wheels, Suzuki's Burgman 400 on 13-inch wheels, and the big Burgman uses a 14-inch rear and 15-inch front combination.

What is the difference (besides looks)? Gyroscopic stability is provided by a spinning large front wheel to steady the scooter. Think of a spinning top as a sideways motorcycle wheel. When the top (wheel) is spinning, the spinning action provides enough gyroscopic stability to keep the top (wheel) balanced on a pivot point (axle). As the top (wheel) slows, it loses gyroscopic stability and falls down. The bigger the top (wheel), the greater the gyroscopic stability.

Thus, big-wheeled scooters like the Beverly and People models have motorcycle-like gyroscopic stability and are much more stable at speed than small-wheeled scooters, but less manuverable at slower speeds. Small-wheeled scooters are more nimble around town but get twitchy at speed. Which is best for you depends on what you value more: manuverability or high-speed stability.

## LAMBRETTA

After decades of the beloved Lambretta marque lying dormant, if not dead, a new Lambretta prototype was unveiled at the 2005 Motorcycle Dealer Expo in Indianapolis. The body will be manufactured in North Carolina, thousands of miles from its Milanese birthplace aside the River Lambro. Classic Motorcycles and Sidecars (CMSI), which also makes the Twist-N-Go scooters, followed the Series III line of Lambrettas in creating a sleek new scooter with many updates. The 12-inch tires will keep the Lammie from tipping, and the liquid-cooled engine will prevent overheating. The kicker for Lambretta loyalists who have spent years waiting is under the side panels: the Piaggio automatic engine.

## MALAGUTI

www.malagutiusa.com

With an obvious hats-off to earlier Italian design, Malaguti unveiled the Yesterday with modern updates such as electronic ignition, no pesky shifting, and a front disc brake that first appeared on the Lambretta. Although the Yesterday may look classic, the fiberglass body and fake spare tire that's

actually a mini glove box reveal a thoroughly modern machine.

The sport scooter in the new Malaguti line is the F12 Phantom Digit. The liquid-cooled 50-cc two-stroke features a sharp F-15-style plastic covering and digital dials on the dashboard, bringing the Phantom into the twenty-first century.

**By today's standards, the handlebars of the Lambretta LD seem rudimentary at best. Still, the mechanical reliability of Innocenti's design has kept this classic scooter on the road. Twist the left grip to change gears (after pulling in the left clutch lever). Giving the right grip a twist gives it gas, and stopping the scooter is done by squeezing the right front brake lever and stomping on the foot brake.**

entered the scooter world for keeps. To prove the longevity of their two-strokes, two French Air Force quarter marshals braved a ride from Saigon to Paris in 1956, arriving down the Champs Elysées to almost as much fanfare as Lindbergh's transatlantic flight from New York. That same year, Peugeot bulked up the wheels' diameter to 10-inches and expanded horsepower.

Peugeot took a hiatus from the scooter world in the 1960s and 1970s, but returned in force in the 1980s with its modern, plastic ST5OL and SC5OL Metropolis models, the Fox, and the Rapido, with red and white two-tone graphics that made up for its lack of rapid speed. The new Scoot'Elec boasts a quiet electric battery that will bring the driver 28 miles from home before needing a recharge (and a ride back). Peugeot offers, among others, the macho-sounding Jet Force Compressor, the Trekker, the Elystar, and the scrappy Speedfight2. While the names evoke gang fighting in the 'hood, Peugeot brags about its Police Patrol Vehicles that are "the number 1 choice for law enforcement organizations."

This Ninja starter bike may sport the latest lines, but the Swedish-colored TGB 303R Laser belies the smaller powerplant hidden beneath the miles of plastic. Smitten scooterists can choose from a two-stroke 50cc or a four-stroke 150cc engine. The latest disc brakes, aluminum wheels, automatic transmission, and Mikuni carb comes standard.

## PEUGEOT
http://www.peugeotmoto.co.uk/
While most scooter manufacturers were looking for a quick buck in what they thought was a scooter gold mine, Peugeot

## STELLA (GENUINE SCOOTER CO.)
www.genuinescooters.com
Seeing the modern market flooded with plastic scooters with retro styling, the Genuine Scooter Company decided to keep

The design of Kymco's Grandvista gives a nod to Darth Vader's storm troopers with its decorative air scoops and grimacing façade. Still, the 250cc liquid-cooled engine enclosed under that La-Z-Boy throne will zip the Grandvista past any vintage runabout.

the old Vespa design and have the scooters stamped in metal by LML in India. Born from Scooterworks in Chicago, Genuine Scooters is a "sister company" to this Vespa shop that has fixed so many quirky two-strokes that it decided to remake a classic that incorporated modern updates. The Stella features fancy Bitubo gas shocks, Grimeca front disc brakes, and the tried-and-true four-speed transmission. This is one of only a handful of modern scooters that does not feature an automatic transmission.

Focusing on the loyal Vespa crowd that desires the bulbous old lines and reliability without the price, the Genuine Scooter Company contracted to have the old Piaggio P series Vespas built again. "Designed with great style in Italy, assembled with great skill in Asia…and sold in the United States by folks who have a love affair with classic scooters," reads the brochure copy.

## VESPA (PIAGGIO)

**www.vespausa.com**
**www.piaggiousa.com**

Piaggio, Vespa's parent company, brought the Vespa brand back to the U.S. market in the late 1990s after a long absence. Vespa purists recoiled at the idea of trying to remake a classic, but the new Vespas keep the curvaceous form of the original, with much of it in metal. Piaggio attempted to cash in on the recent Tuscany craze by reminding customers that its factory is near Pisa, and by offering Tuscan color schemes: Giotto Orange, Olive Green, Livorno Blue, and Etruscan Red. Piaggio hasn't been sitting on its collective hands during its absence from the American market in the 1980s and 1990s, but has continued to iron out its scooters' shortcomings.

The "wasp" reentered the U.S. market with a bang at the end of the last millennium with Vespa boutiques opening across the United States. Piaggio insisted these dealers open only in major metropolitan areas and sell only Vespas. The slick new Vespa was high-priced compared to the competition, but its name made customers line up to get the coolest new ride in town. Two basic models were offered, the ET2 with a 50-cc engine (the first fuel-injected two-stroke in the world, according to Piaggio) and luxurious electric starter, and the 150-cc ET4 four-stroke .

The top-of-the-line Vespa is the ET4 Granturismo released in 2003. The 200-cc engine on 12-inch wheels makes for a speedy, sturdy ride.

Piaggio also sells a complete line of Piaggio-badged scooters, ranging from 50-cc air-cooled traditional scooters to 460-cc maxi scoots. Piaggio's Beverly (BV in the U.S. market) line features 16-inch wheels that provide more high-speed stability than the traditional small wheels.

## SUZUKI

**www.suzuki.com**

As one of the classic Japanese manufacturers, Suzuki kept out of the scooter market until it offered its 50-cc Address model in Japan

The eGO fudges the line between scooters and mopeds with a handy step-through design and borrows the no-slip safety strips from a bathtub to mount on the plastic floorboard. One brake lever controls both brakes—the front being a high-tech disc.

Italy's two most famous exports are united at last: scooters and pizza. The TGB Delivery Scooter replaces the passenger with a handy 150 liter box for carrying pepperoni to famished frat boys.

The Burgman 400 is possibly the most popular scooter in the U.S. market, and with good reason. For many it is the perfect compromise between a traditional scooter and a maxi scooter. The 385-cc engine produces enough horsepower to propel a solo rider in excess of 100 miles per hour if the conditions are right, yet the handling is agile enough so that the riding experience is closer to a traditional scooter than it is to the "super-maxi" maxi scooters, the Silver Wing and the Burgman 650. The Burgman has spawned a loyal following as fanatical about its chosen ride as any Lambretta or Vespa crowd.

### TN'G (TWIST N' GO)
**www.tngscooters.com**
Classic Motorcycles & Sidecars began this upstart scooter company to ride the new craze by straddling the two types of buyers: speedsters and modsters. Painted in mother-of-barstool gray, the Del Rey has the downward tilt of a sportbike, but its oversized nose looks like it got popped one at the local watering hole. The Del Rey sports a 125-cc four-stroke engine with front disc brake to stop the speed. The 49-cc LS is a mini version of the Del Rey, with menacing black-and-red two-tone.

For those who opt for fashion over function, Twist 'N Go features its Italian city lineup: Venice, Milano, or Verona. The most popular, Venice, comes with a 49-cc engine. The Milano offers the choice of a 50-cc, 125-cc, or 150-cc power plant. The 150-cc Verona has larger wheels for a smooth ride on the lengthier wheelbase.

### YAMAHA
**www.yamaha-motor.com**
In 1993, Yamaha debuted its Frog scooter with retro-chic styling. Powered by a 250-cc four-stroke engine, it was dressed in snappy two-tone livery with dual frog-eye headlamps.

In 1996, one of Yamaha's first maxi-scooters hit the showroom. The 250-cc Majesty had more boxy lines than its competitors but boasted a four-stroke, liquid-cooled engine.

By 2004, Yamaha offered the classic-looking Vino and Vino Classic scooter in four-stroke 125-cc and two-stroke 50-cc versions. The Vino "makes you look like you just rolled out of a Fellini movie, and actually makes getting around town fun

**Scooterworks of Chicago kept countless Vespas running when Piaggio wouldn't import their scooters into the U.S. After years of wrenching the capricious scooters into shape, their mechanics knew what foibles to fix if they were ever to design their own. Enter Stella stage left. The Genuine Scooter Company took the sleek Italian design of the P-Series Vespa and ironed out the wrinkles.**

and Europe in the 1990s. The Burgman line of scooters, offered in 2004 with either a 645-cc or 385-cc four-stroke engine, comprises Suzuki's entry into the U.S. market. Weighing in at 524 pounds and 405 pounds respectively, these space-age, plastic scooters feature disc brakes and adjustable shocks. The Burgman 650 offers a feature to let the driver choose between normal and power automatic modes with the touch of a finger.

While the Kymco Vitality has a sporty bench seat, the 50cc engine leaves a void of power for the pillion and makes a passenger into contraband in most regions.

instead of frustrating," read the brochure copy, with an obvious reference to Paparazzo in *La Dolce Vita*, and the mechanical breakdowns of loyal Vespa riders everywhere. For riders more concerned with performance than looking like a Cine Città extra, Yamaha built the two-stroke Zuma with dual headlights. The high-performance Zuma, for a relatively economical price, has made this reliable scooter a favorite for the speedster who is looking for a starter motorcycle.

## MODERN SCOOTS

In general, the rules for buying a used modern scooter are about the same as those for buying any other type of used vehicle. The outer appearance is generally a good indication of the inner condition because a rider who cared for a scooter's appearance most likely cared for its mechanical parts, too. If a scooter looks like a refugee from the set of a Michael Bay film, politely thank the seller for his time and walk away.

With scooters, a buyer has the advantage of the fact that most scooters have relatively low mileage. This means that the working parts have received little wear and tear. The downside of low mileage is that a scooter might have sat unused for a long a time and may have problems with seals drying up, cracking, and leaking. Check around the engine, clutch, and final drive for greasy spots that might suggest oil seepage. Even if you find evidence,

changing most seals is not a huge undertaking, but you will want to figure the expense of such work into the price you offer the seller.

Another problem that crops up when a scooter has sat unused is a buildup of fuel residue in the carburetor, gas tank, or

Following the lead of Italjet's Velocifero that brought back the bulbous early Vespa lines, TN'G released the two-tone 50cc Venice for scooter buffs who like the classic feel. Never mind that no scooters inhabit the island of Venice and clandestine putt-putts would be thrown into the canal or the Doge's dungeon.

The perfect ride for zooming by the paparazzi on Via Montenapoleone or dodging the latest Communist strike in Piazza del Duomo, TN'G's Milano has a peppy four-stroke 125cc engine to beat out the latest Ferrari Modena at the stop light. The stealth black paint scheme may not keep the Milano off of police radar, but at least it matches the latest Armani wardrobe.

fuel-injection system. This is especially problematic in areas where the fuel is oxygenated with a product like ethanol. This can be avoided by using a product like Stabil Fuel Stabilizer when storing a scooter. Better yet, find a station that sells non-oxygenated fuel for collectible vehicles and small engines, then use Stabil. If a scooter that has sat unused for an extended period isn't running properly, a gunked-up fuel system is a likely culprit. If you are comfortable rebuilding a carb or fuel-injection system, this is not a huge problem. If not, it can mean expensive repairs and should be avoided. If the scooter runs and carburets well, there is likely no problem

Another glitch that could crop up may involve the electrical system. This tends to be more of a problem with Italian scooters than Japanese. If it is a small scooter with a kick starter, a weak charging system isn't a huge problem. If a scooter lacks a kick starter and has a tendency towards electrical problems, you might want to carry around a set of jumper cables. If you buy a scooter and find the battery tends to run down easily, even after replacing the battery, you will want to invest in a trickle charger that you will use when your scooter sits for an extended period.

Be skeptical of any modifications a previous owner has made. A Zuma bored

out to 80-cc with a titanium expansion chamber and a racing clutch kit might be a rocket when you first buy it, but if the owner hasn't properly geared the oil pump (which is almost certainly the case) it will only be a rocket for only a few miles. After that it will be an expensive overhaul project patiently waiting for you to find the time and resources for a complete engine rebuild. Whatever you do, don't pay extra for such modifications since they detract from the scooters value, they don't add to it.

When buying a used Japanese scooter, there are not many problems to worry about. Like a Honda Accord or Toyota Camry, most Japanese scooters are as reliable as an anvil. Provided they haven't been crashed, raced, or heavily modified, they should be almost as trouble-free as a new scooter.

The same is true of Italian scooters—a used Italian scooter should be as reliable as a new Italian scooter. This doesn't mean it will be trouble-free, since statistically you're much more likely to have problems with a new Italian scooter than a new Japanese scooter. The flip side is that Italian scooters are, almost without exception, much more stylish than Japanese scooters, which tend to have frumpy lines and come in drab colors. Italian scooters tend to be beautifully sculpted and come in vibrant colors. So you pick your compromise: outstanding reliability and less-than-exciting styling, or high style and spotty reliability.

A couple of new Japanese scooters offer the best of both worlds—Yamaha's Morphous and Suzuki's sporty Burgman 400S—but you are unlikely to find those on the used scooter market.

Scooters built in Asia can be a mixed bag. Kymco has been around a long time and has earned a reputation for building reliable scooters. Some of the other scooters built in China and Korea can have dubious reliability. If you've never heard of the brand, beware. There are a lot of companies in Asia building scooters, and not all are building good ones.

## CLASSIC SCOOTS

Many scooterists who are looking for a used bike go for the classic, or at least something close. Vespas are the preferred bike, but Lambrettisti argue that their scooter has

## WORDS TO THE WISE
### BEFORE BUYING: INTROSPECTIVE CONSUMERISM

Before being exposed to a lineup of beautiful, candy-red putt-putts, consider these questions to avoid future buyer's remorse:

• **How far will you drive it?** Buying a classic certainly gives you street cred, but unless you're mechanically inclined, or can afford a good mechanic you should stick with the modern scoots.

• **How fast do you want to go?** If you're going to drive only on city roads, 30–35 miles per hour might be enough. A 50-cc scooter will easily hit those speeds. The advantage is a moped license might only be required (check the laws of your state—licensing requirements vary widely from state to state). Usually, passengers aren't allowed on 50-cc scooters, however, spoiling the whole point of the bench seat.

• **Will you go on the highway?** If you want to go on the highway, a 200-cc scooter is recommended to exceed speeds of 55 miles per hour and safely pass cars (again, check your local laws—some states ban vehicles under a certain engine displacement on freeways).

• **Will you commute, or ride just for fun?** If you just want to cruise around the lake on Saturday afternoon, a vintage bike could be perfect (with a bit of elbow grease). If you must show up for your job at 8:00 a.m. or risk the unemployment line, a slick new scooter may be the ticket.

• **Are spare parts available?** Consider how long the brand has been for sale in your area. Unusual vintage bikes were often imported in such small numbers that finding parts off of old scooters is a constant quest. Research their availability before taking the leap. Even with newer bikes, parts availability might be an issue. If a company is unable to maintain a functioning website in your market, or if it hasn't updated its website for more than a couple of years, it might not have the resources to get you the parts you need should your scooter break down.

• **What gadgets do you want?** Modern scooters offer electric ignition, disc brakes, automatic transmission, and even cell phone rechargers. While some of the modern technology makes for a smoother ride, remember that each extra bell and whistle can break. In general, the fewer electrical parts a scooter has (especially an Italian scooter), the less there is to go wrong.

• **What do your friends recommend?** Ask fellow scooterists what they would advise based on their experience. Brand loyalty often clouds good judgment, but word of mouth

is more valuable than a salesman's pitch. Be especially skeptical of a person with his or her preferred make tattooed on their bicep. Make friends with the folks at your local scooter shop and find out the quirks and foibles of your favorite bikes.

## SECOND-HAND SCOOTS

From war-torn classic to gently used, you're likely to find scooters in various states of disrepair when shopping for a ride. When looking for a used scooter, you will find everything from low-mile current models to basket cases that need complete restoration. Honestly assess your needs and abilities and financial resources when deciding how much of a fixer-upper you want to buy. A nearly-new, low-mileage Burgman 400 will cost almost as much as a new scooter, but it may be cheaper than trying to restore some arcane vintage scooter. Some scooter shops restore classic bikes for sale or will sell fixer-uppers. Project bikes are not recommended for first time scooter buyers unless you have a lot of free time, friends who know how to help you, and a good line on spare parts.

Used prices are whatever the market will bear. With some vintage scooters selling for far more than their original sale price, scooter seekers have scoured small towns in search of the Lammies and Vespas distributed by Montgomery Ward and Sears. When you buy a beautifully rebuilt Lambretta for more than a thousand dollars, be prepared for fellow scooterists telling tales of how they discovered a similar bike for less than a hundred bucks (and what a fool you've been). Rebut by asking how much time and money they spent on repairing the bike. Watch them hem and haw and say how much they learned, how fun it was, and other such excuses.

The success of the Kymco People prompted an ever-expanding engine. This brand new 250cc four-stroke now propels the scooterist past 80 mph, according to Kymco literature. Works racers testing the People in wind tunnels under ideal conditions needn't stop on a dime, however. Luckily, Kymco plopped a pair of disc brakes on the front and back 16-inch wheels.

While the name "People" will hardly go down in the annals of brilliant scooter nomenclature, Kymco's leading scooter hit a nerve. Most wannabe scooterists didn't want a mini donor bike decked out in neon, but they longed for a vintage-style scooter that they didn't have to wrench at the side of the road. The People—along with the Velocifero, the Vino, the new Vespa, and the Scarabeo—answered their prayers.

more refined lines (and a more stable ride). Beyond the experience of these two makes, a whole world of little-known putt-putts presents itself. The Brits made the Bond, the Dayton, the cigar-shaped Piatti, and the gorgeous Triumph/BSA scooter. The Germans produced solid scooters like the Dürkopp, Heinkel, Maico, NSU, and Zündapp. The Italians dreamed of more than Vespas and Lambrettas and sold Aermacchi, Ducati, Iso, Laverda, MV Agusta, Parilla, Rumi, and many more speedy scoots that only Italian design could create. The French made the outrageous and intensely

creative Bernadet and Terrot scooters that would leave any collector slack-jawed. On the other side of the world, the Japanese invented some sleek scooters (before the plastic revolution) including the Fuji Rabbit, the early Honda Juno, and the Mitsubishi Silver Pigeon. Stateside, the earliest scooter revolution fostered makes like Crocker, Cushman, Doodlebug, Harley-Davidson, Mead, Motoscoot, Mustang, and Salsbury. The world of collectible scooters is only limited by the pocketbook and space in the garage. See the "Modern or Vintage?" sidebar for more advice on deciding whether you're an ideal candidate for a classic scoot.

For buyers of the two most popular used scooters, however, here's a run down of most Lambrettas and Vespas.

## LAMBRETTA LD

The LD was the first Lambretta widely distributed in the United States. Four versions of the shaft-drive LD were sold: the LD 125 from 1951 to 1956; the LD 150 from 1954 to 1957; the LD 125/57 from 1955 to 1958; and the LD 150/57 from 1957 to 1958. Electric start was optional on the LD 125 and LD 150 models.

## LAMBRETTA TV 175 SERIES 1

TV stood for "Turismo Veloce," or "Touring Speed," a scaled-down translation of *gran turismo* into scooter-speak. The

Scooter showrooms offer a wide variety of wares. The vintage-looking scooters in the background are actually modern Stellas from Genuine Scooter Company of Chicago.

The 49cc Ducati Phantom takes the ideals of a high-performance motorcycle of this Bologna-based brand and squeezes it into a scooter. The question is whether Ducati would ever lower itself to allow a scooter into its state-of-the-art motorcycle museum in Emilia-Romagna.

The Phantom displays a very sportbike-like rear end.

TV1 was built from 1957 to 1958 and the shaft-drive of all earlier Lambrettas was shelved in place of a radically modern, enclosed duplex chain drive that required no adjustment, lubrication, or cleaning.

## LAMBRETTA LI 150 AND LI 125 SERIES 1

In early 1958 and until 1959, Innocenti built its new Li line based on a completely new engine from the preceding TV. It was modern, powerful, and reliable whereas the TV1 was modern, powerful, and

fragile. The Li line would dictate the direction of Lambretta scooters until 1971 when Innocenti halted production—and even then Serveta (in Spain) and Scooters India would continue building Li and Li-based models.

## LAMBRETTA TV 175 SERIES 2

The TV1 was pulled out of production at the end of 1958 to be replaced by the TV2, which was a new scooter based not on the TV1 but on the successful Li line. Highly recommended.

## LAMBRETTA LI 150 AND LI 125 SERIES 2

Along with the TV2, the Li line was modified in 1959 with the headlamp moved from the apron to the handlebars, creating a much more stylish scooter.

## LAMBRETTA LI 125 AND 150 SERIES 3

At the end of 1961, the bodywork of the Li and TV lines were redrawn for the Li Series 3. The new "Slimline" styling was sleek and angular with flash replacing the fleshy look of the earlier Lambrettas. The Slimline replaced the curvaceous Marilyn-Monroe styling that characterized the 1950s Lambrettas with the thinner Twiggy look of the 1960s.

## LAMBRETTA TV 175 SERIES 3

The Lambretta TV introduced the disc brake to scootering and even influenced motorcycle and car manufacturers in the 1960s to adopt this radical braking system.

## LAMBRETTA GT 200

Built from 1963 to 1965, the Gran Turismo 200 was essentially a hot-rodded 200-cc TV3 able to top 70 miles per hour.

## LAMBRETTA 150 LI SPECIAL PACEMAKER, 125 LI SPECIAL; 150 AND 200 SPECIAL X (SX)

Built to match the *Turismo Veloce* Lambrettas, the Li Special and Special X Series were performance versions of the basic line that ran from 1963 through 1969.

## VESPA 125 AND 150

The earliest Vespas brought into the United States were the "Fenderlights" or "Handlebar" versions. The wheels of these early Vespas were a puny eight inches in diameter, which caused relatively unstable handling.

The Ferrari-red mixed with Ducati's tell-tale dual headlamps make this the perfect starter crotch rocket.

Industrial meets digital with this slick dashboard.

## VESPA 150 AND 160 GS

Introduced in 1954, the 150 GS came with a bench seat for two people and was available exclusively in metallic grey. The 160 GS was introduced in 1962. Distinguishing features of the 160 were the added metal trim on the front fender, a mat on the center bridge, a smaller saddle seat with glove box behind it instead of in the left side panel, and a new exhaust system.

## VESPA 150 GL

In 1962, the 150 Gran Lusso, with two saddle seats, was announced. Although not quite as sporty as the GS, the GL sat atop more stable 10-inch wheels than the previous Vespa 150's 8-inchers.

## VESPA 50, 50 N, 50 S, 50 L, 50 N SPECIAL, 50 N ELESTART, AND 50 SPRINTER

The "Vespina" (or little Vespa) debuted in 1963. By 1993, with a revised 50-cc 50S Vintage and 50A with automatic transmission still in production, more than four million 50-cc Vespas had been built.

## VESPA 180 SS

The engine from the 1964 160 GS was enlarged to make the 181.1-cc Super Sport, which replaced the GS as the top-of-the-line Vespa.

When metallic green Vespas were sold throughout Europe in the 1950s, ambitious scooterists used the pokey little putt-putts to criss-cross the continent in search of greener grass. Piaggio's new top-of-the-line Vespa, the Granturismo, gives these scooterists filled with wanderlust a more reliable ride to complete the Grand Tour of Naples, Rome, Florence and Venice atop two wheels.

## VESPA 90, 90SS, AND 50SS

In 1964, Piaggio developed the 90 as a middle ground between the SS and 125 models and the glorified moped 50-cc scooters.

## VESPA 150 SPRINT, 150 SPRINT VELOCE, VESPA 125 SUPER, AND 150 SUPER

In 1965, the Vespa 150 Sprint VLB replaced the 150 GL. Four-speed transmission was standard by now, as well as the bench seat.

## VESPA 125 PRIMAVERA AND 125 ET3

In 1965, the 50-cc engine of the 50SS was enlarged to 125-cc but kept in the 50 chassis to create the 125 Primavera (or Spring). In 1967, the Primavera became the ET3. The ET3 was so popular Piaggio revived the model for the 1980s and 1990s as the ET3 Vintage.

## VESPA 125 GT AND 125 GTR

In 1969, Piaggio announced yet another version of its 125 —the Gran Turismo—that had essentially the same motor as the 125 Super with higher compression adding to its velocity.

## VESPA 180 RALLY 1968, RALLY 200, AND RALLY 200 ELECTRONIC

In the late 1960s, Piaggio created a new speedster, the Rally 200. The Rally was the hot Vespa of the day, and Piaggio boasted the Rally as the most reliable Vespa thus far, making it perfect for long distance touring.

## VESPA 100 SPORT

This small frame scooter from 1978 had the updated 12-volt electrical system, but still had the three-speed gearbox of the V90.

## VESPA PX 125, 150, AND 200E

In 1977, the P Series was the brainchild of Piaggio's managing director, Ing. Giovanni Squazzini. The P stood for Piaggio, the X for extra qualities, and the E for electronic ignition.

The bulbous behind is back with Piaggio's updated Vespa. Argh! Don't tell me that's an oil slick under the floorboard. After all, it is Italian.

## VESPA PK 50S, 80S, 80E, 125S, 125E, PX150E, AND PX200E

The PK models were introduced in 1983 and all had four-speed automatic transmissions. Piaggio offered the PX series with a four-speed manual transmission as well. The PX200E continued through 1993 (but not in the United States) with the remainder of the Piaggio Vespa line made up of the 50A automatic, 50S Vintage, 100 Vintage, 125A automatic, and 125ET3 Vintage

## HOW DO I DRIVE THIS THING? SHIFTING, TURNING, AND BRAKING LIKE A PRO

Riding a scooter is fun, but it is also serious business with potentially serious consequences. Too often people think the fun aspect somehow negates the dangerous, but that is simply not the case. The same physics apply to crashing a scooter as crashing a motorcycle. If you fall down you are probably going to get hurt. But there are steps you can take to ensure that you don't fall down or, if you do fall, to minimize the hurt.

Your best bet to avoid pain is to avoid falling down, and the best way not to crash is to develop your riding skills.

To increase your odds of living to be a ripe old scooter rider, take a Motorcycle Safety Foundation's Basic RiderCourse, or the MSF's BRC, for those of you who dig acronyms. In the next chapter you will learn more about the MSF. For now you should just know that you will need to take this course. It really is the best and safest way to learn to ride a two-wheeler.

Learning to ride a scooter is an important task that is too complex to adequately cover in one short section. An excellent book devoted to learning to ride motorcycles is appropriately titled *How to Ride a Motorcycle*, by Pat Hahn (Motorbooks, 2005). This book should be considered an essential part of your riding kit, like a helmet, gloves, and boots.

The fundamentals of riding covered in *How to Ride a Motorcycle* are as true of scooters as they are of any other motorized two-wheeler (with the exception of the Segue), but there are some eccentricities about riding a scooter that are not covered in Pat Hahn's book or the other riding books available. While a complete syllabus for a course on riding scooters is beyond the scope of this book, you need to understand

a few of the peculiarities of scooter riding to properly develop scooter riding skills.

• **Starting.** One of the main differences between scooters and other motorcycles is that most modern scooters have automatic transmissions. This means that they do not follow the starting procedure of a regular motorcycle, almost all of which have manual transmissions.

All scooters with automatic transmissions follow a variation of the same starting procedure. It isn't unlike starting a car with an automatic transmission. First, you either need to put the bike on the centerstand or support it with your legs and lift the sidestand. Most scooters won't start with the sidestand down. Then, firmly grab one of the brake levers—this is the equivalent of putting a car with an automatic transmission in park and is required to engage the starter on most modern scooters—and press the starter button. Some scooters still have a choke, or a fast-idle lever if they are fuel injected, but most modern scooters are like modern automobiles and have no choke. If

Piaggio's premier putt-putt, the Granturismo, may no longer be Corradino d'Ascanio's scooter for the masses, but who needs comradery if your scooter doesn't stall? Finally, Vespa ironed out its persistent foibles with the Granturismo, but high quality totes a hefty price tag.

Looking less like Honda's famous barcalounger Helix scooter but not as motorcycle-like as the Gold Wing, Honda's Silver Wing walks the line between scooter and cycle.

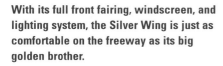

With its full front fairing, windscreen, and lighting system, the Silver Wing is just as comfortable on the freeway as its big golden brother.

the scooter is running properly, it should start right up.

Starting a scooter with a manual transmission and a kickstarter is a bit more complicated, but it is also more like a standard motorcycle. Make sure your scooter is in neutral and the choke is on. If your dashboard lights don't tell you, rock the scooter forward and backward to see if it moves smoothly, which indicates you're in neutral.

To kick-start your scooter, most bikes require that you push it forward off the centerstand. Make sure the scooter is in neutral and the choke is on (if a scooter has an automatic transmission, you can bet dollars to donuts that it will still have a choke or fast-idle lever). Make sure the sole of your right shoe is dry to avoid slipping, and put it on the kick starter. While holding the handlebars tightly, push down hard and fast on the kick starter. Repeat until the engine starts and twist the throttle to give it enough gas to stay running. Turn off the choke in a couple of minutes. If these two techniques don't work, you probably should clean the plugs, check the gas, or adjust the carburetor. Remind yourself that this is part of the vintage scooter experience.

• **Shifting.** If you have an automatic, consider yourself lucky that you don't have to constantly switch gears. If not, it will take a bit of practice to master the technique of shifting, which differs quite a bit from a standard motorcycle because the shifter is usually on the left handgrip like a bicycle rather than down by the left foot.

To shift into first gear, pull in the clutch (usually the left handlebar lever) and gently twist the grip forward so the "1" lines up with the little arrow. Slowly release the clutch and twist the throttle a bit (the right handle). With a bit of practice, you'll become accustomed to the exact point where the clutch and gears engage. Give just

enough gas to avoid stalling the engine, and avoid revving the engine unnecessarily.

To shift into second, let off the gas, pull in the clutch, twist the left grip backwards until the "2" lines up with the arrow. Slowly release the clutch and give it gas. Continue to third and fourth gear as you speed up.

• **Downshifting.** Modern motor manufacturers often recommend against downshifting, advising you to rely more on the brakes with the argument that brake pads are easier to replace than the gearbox and clutch. Regardless, knowing how to slow down gradually by downshifting can help avoid locking up the brakes or stopping too suddenly on an oil patch.

Downshifting into first is nearly impossible and is likely to stop you too suddenly. Don't downshift when going too fast in any gear as this can dramatically slow you down and could effectively lock up your rear tire. When in a higher gear (third or fourth), let off the gas for a few seconds, pull in the clutch, twist the left handle to the next lowest gear (second or third). As you let out the clutch, give just a little bit of gas to ease into the downshift.

• **Braking.** More important than learning to move your scooter is knowing

how to stop. Again, this differs from standard motorcycles of the type covered in riding books and used in the MSF BRC. On most scooters equipped with automatic transmissions, both brake levers are on the handlebars. The front brake is in the same position as on motorcycles (right front handlebar), but the rear brake is on the left handlebar, where the clutch resides on a motorcycle. (On scooters with manual transmissions the arrangement is more like that of a traditional motorcycle, with the right handlebar lever controlling the front brake, the left handlebar lever controlling the clutch, and a foot pedal for the rear brake).

The brake arrangement on an automatic scooter is the cause of many accidents; when experienced motorcyclists get on a scooter they forget that the left handlebar lever is not the clutch. Instinctively they pull in the "clutch" lever to change gears and lock up the rear brake.

On single-tracked, two-wheeled vehicles, there is not a lot of rubber contacting the road at any given time, meaning there is only a limited amount of traction avaible. This makes it easy to lock up the brakes and, consequently, to crash.

**The Silver Wing also sports a full motorcycle-style instrument panel.**

## WORDS TO THE WISE
### MODERN OR VINTAGE? A BUYER'S GUIDE BY STEPHEN HELLER

Everyone loves the cachet of pulling up to a bar on his or her vintage Vespa or Lambretta, but a classic bike may not be for everyone. Unquestionably there will be a time where you will be stuck somewhere with a nonrunning scooter. Will you pull off the cowl and dig in? Or will you call AAA? If your answer is the latter, then a new bike will be your best bet.

If you are buying new, there are a few different options that you can get with the "retro" look: Vespa PX150, Genuine Scooters' Stella, and the Bajaj Chetak. These three 150-cc scooters have manual transmissions with the shifting and the clutch on the handlebars—as retro as you can get without the 20-plus-year-old headaches. The PX and Stella are virtually identical to the earlier two-stroke P-series Vespas that were sold into the early 1980s in the United States, but with a few additions. Both scoots have a front disc brake; the PX has a halogen headlight, while the Stella has gas-filled shocks and a reed valve on the engine to help with gas mileage. The Chetak is a bit different style-wise, has a cleaner-running four-stroke engine, and is the only one of the

three available in California because of emissions standards.

Many scooter manufacturers also offer automatic transmission scooters with classic style in a broad range of engine capacities, from the 50-cc Kymco People to the 500-cc Aprilia Atlantic.

When it comes to choosing an automatic—or any type of scooter—a major point to look for is the quality of the manufacturer and the availability of parts. You don't want a scooter that has bolts falling off as you go down the road and then, to add insult to injury, find you are unable to replace those parts. To combat this, do research on the scooter you are planning on purchasing and buy the scooter through a reputable dealer. (Read: Not out of a neighbor's garage or through an auto parts store.)

The next step is to find a scooter with a style that fits your body. Not all scooters are manufactured for every body style. A 6-foot, 4-inch male will not fit on the same scooter as a 5-foot, 4-inch female. So go to a dealer and sit on as many scooters as possible and find one you can ride and hold up comfortably.

---

Avoiding locking up the brakes should be a top priority for a scooter rider who values his or her hide.

Scooters need the power of both front and rear brakes to stop in the least amount of time. Apply both of your brakes at the same time and remember that about three quarters of your braking power is in the front brake. You won't flip over your handlebars if you use the front brake.

Give yourself plenty of room to stop, if possible, to avoid locking up the brakes. If you feel the front wheel lock up, immediately let off the brake for an instant

Slapping a two-tone paint scheme on the scooter side panels, horn cover, and handlebars owes styling kudos to GM's Harley Earl in his ever-expanding quest to get away from Henry Ford's "any color as long as it's black" credo. The Mods specialized in following Earl's lead by screwing on as much chrome and paint as their scooter canvas would allow. Here, a modern Vespa is decked out in a questionable pink-and-white two tone.

and then reapply it. If you lock the rear tire, try to reapply the brake. If you find yourself skidding, try to steer in the direction of the skid. For example, if you're leaning to the right and skidding to the left, turn the wheel slightly to the left. If you find yourself in this position, you are likely to be testing your safety gear very shortly and will be glad you bought a quality helmet. If you do keep the scooter on two wheels after going into a skid, treat yourself to something nice to celebrate a great save.

If you're braking and hit a patch of oil or sand and feel one of the wheels lock up, instantly let up on the brakes. Reapply the brakes once you're past the bad patch. The same applies for spinning the rear wheel on a slippery patch. Let up on the gas until you've cleared the area. If you're going slow enough, remember you can always use the Fred Flintstone technique with your trusty feet.

Proper braking technique is discussed at length in Pat Hahn's book *How to Ride a Motorcycle*. While the controls may differ, the physics stay the same, so the techniques discussed in that book can save your bacon on a scooter as well as on a motorcycle.

• **Turning.** Going around a corner on a scooter is a nothing like turning in an automobile. While a car's steering wheel is rotated a full turn, scooters' handlebars will only be turned slightly to go around the same curve. Just like turning a bicycle, you must lean into the turn. However, don't let the scooter lean down too much while you stay perpendicular to the ground. Lean with the scooter. Before entering the turn, let off on the gas to slow down a bit. Once in the turn, avoid shifting or braking. Keep the gas flow steady and accelerate a bit around the end of the turn to ride like a true pro.

Again, this is discussed in detail in *How to Ride a Motorcycle*.

• **Parking.** Most scooters have a centerstand that you pull down with the heel of your shoe. The centerstand is a U-shaped rod that folds down from under the motorcycle and lifts the rear wheel off the ground with two pads or "feet", thus supporting the motorcycle while you leave it unattended.

Using the centerstand requires a bit of practice. Give yourself plenty of room behind you (at least 18 inches). Once the

Upping the ante against rival Japanese company Honda, Suzuki released its Burgman with a 638cc engine that is weighty competition for the 582cc Silver Wing and makes the new Vespa look positively sluggish.

Perhaps seeing the Vespa clones like Stella of Genuine Scooter Company and the Chetak of Bajaj, Piaggio sought to bring back the true Vespa that it made famous. The PX 150 (pictured here in a limited edition for the American market) keeps the classic lines of the P-series that began in 1977 in Pontedera, Italy.

Piaggio released the Vespa PX150 in the U.S. nearly twenty years after it left the American market due to fears of product liability laws. Now, the Italian company has met with a new dilemma when its PX-series scooters can't meet the stringent environmental standards of California, making it unavailable to cruise the Hollywood hills.

two feet of the centerstand are on terra firma, grab the handlebar with one hand and a secure portion of the rear of the scooter with the other. Most modern scooters have a grab rail of some type conveniently located for this task. Next, push down with your foot while you lift with your hands (this is the act that actually lifts the scooter off the ground) and rock the scooter back onto the stand. This little maneuver is more difficult than it first appears, especially if you do it wrong. If you do it right, it's not that difficult.

If your scooter has a side kickstand, make sure you balance the bike carefully and that the kickstand is on hard ground. Beware hot asphalt and soft ground! The metal from the centerstand can slowly sink into the asphalt or soft earth and you may return to a sadly tipped scooter. This can be avoided by placing a flattened can or a similar flat object under the stand.

Weighing in at double most scooters' load, the Yamaha Majesty needs its 400cc engine to push it along with a passenger with ease.

Taking a classic, even iconic, symbol such as the Vespa and updating it to modern specifications was no easy task. When the new ET2 and ET4 scooters hit the piazza, Italians knew that it was still a Vespa. Finally, Piaggio updated its little engines to be available as a (somewhat) environmentally-friendly four-stroke motor in the ET4.

# SAFETY—START SEEING SCOOTERS!

## Chapter 3

When you take an MSF RiderCourse, you will learn how not to ride like this.

### WHAT YOU WILL LEARN

- There is no Italian word for "safe"
- How Isaac Newton can save you from a hospital visit
- The importance of safety gear
- How to ride in a rally without wiping out
- Techniques for avoiding facial road rash
- How to drive like Michael Schumacher on a scooter

Safety is the inherent human desire not to scrape one's knees. Problems can arise, however, if a new rider hops on a scooter and throws away all common sense. Absolute speed blinds absolutely.

"Safe? We don't have this word in Italian," said a friend from Modena, land of Lamborghini, Maserati, and Ferrari. "We say *sicuro*, but that's 'secure.' Nothing can be 'safe' because everything is dangerous." Obviously, these are not the people you want driving your taxicab or giving advice on scooter safety. When Piaggio and Innocenti introduced their scooters into America, Cushman was already king of the market and had an equally thrilling, if risky, scooter to drive. Product liability laws were science fiction, and it was left to the media to warn consumers of the danger in scootering.

"The makers of Vespas and Lambrettas, the two major Italian makes, use economy and maneuverability as their two main selling points. For many people, these are enough to make up for their relative lack of comfort…. Scooters are inherently unstable, like spin-ning tops…. On a scooter you lean over, and there you are, upside down in the ditch. You have to influence the scooter around a corner in a series of more or less controlled wobbles." According to *Atlantic Monthly*, July 1962

A 1958 *New York Times Magazine* article was a little kinder, but obviously delirious: "These machines have a low center of gravity and if they fall over you're right there on the ground. Safer than if an accident happens in a closed car." Obviously the wise scribe who penned these words had never fallen over on a scooter and had failed to take into account how an auto's body can actually shield the driver. Hitting the ground at 40 miles per hour is more than enough to land you in the morgue.

Few scooterists donned a helmet in the 1950s, but now we know better. Sure, there's nothing better than the freedom of riding with the wind in your hair, at least until you have your first scooter scare. A field trip to the emergency room on a

# le Scooter

LE DISPENSAIRE

80ᶠ

Saturday night will convince even the most hesitant scooterist to pop on a helmet, provided he or she is lucky enough to survive the mishap.

Helmets range from the novelty ones worn by people in protest of ones laws to full-faced helmets of the type used by professional racers and many motorcyclists. The novelty helmets are jokes, providing about as much protection as a plastic Mardi Gras hat, and should never be worn under any circumstances. You'll definitely want to wear a helmet approved by the Department of Transportation (DOT). You can identify these helmets by the white sticker with black letters reading "DOT."

Disregarding the novelty "beanie" helmets with fake DOT stickers, you will find three basic types of helmets: half helmets, three-quarter helmets, and full-face helmets.

## HALF HELMETS

Half helmets offer the minimum amount of cranial protection acceptable to the DOT. Imagine cutting a bowling ball in half or wearing a pudding bowl on your head, and you'll get an idea about what a half helmet looks like. A halfhelmet is designed to

*"Scooters are inherently unstable, like spinning tops.... On a scooter you lean over, and there you are, upside down in the ditch. You have to influence the scooter around a corner in a series of more or less controlled wobbles."*
—Atlantic Monthly, *July, 1962*

## WORDS TO THE WISE
## HELMET HEAD: COVER THAT NOGGIN

Motorcycle riders have effectively lobbied legislators to let them keep the wind in their hair. These are motorcyclists who have never been in a serious accident. Consider that Italy—land of Lambretta, Vespa, Italjet, Aprilia, and countless other scooter brands—now requires that all scooterists, motorcyclists, and moped riders wear a helmet.

Don't believe the false rumors that a helmet impairs your vision, can break your neck in an accident, or mutes hearing. When considering a full-face helmet or a pudding-basin half-helmet, remember the old axiom, "A half-helmet will save your skull and a full-face helmet will save your face."

Most accidents happen within a mile of your house—because that's where you'll be doing most of your riding. Therefore, even zipping up to the Quickie Mart for some milk should require a helmet. Wearing a helmet on longer rides reduces fatigue, keeps the bugs from your teeth, and protects your eyes from the wind. An added benefit of wearing a helmet is when the local police pull you over, they'll recognize that you're at least somewhat responsible.

The helmet should be snug but comfortable. Scooter helmets have been developed specifically to protect your skull, thanks to the polycarbonate outer shell and the impact-absorbing liner of polystyrene.

Leaving the straps undone is definitely cool, but makes the helmet worthless. If you're flung over your handlebars, the helmet will probably be shot from your head like a cannonball and leave your scalp open to the elements.

protect the basic brain structures from impact during a crash, but will do little to protect your face. These are better than no helmet at all, and are the choice of many scooter riders because they offer the classic look of a traditional pudding-bowl helmet, but the other choices offer significantly more protection.

### THREE-QUARTER OR OPEN-FACE HELMETS

Three-quarter or open-face helmets are similar to half helmets except that they extend down on the sides to cover the rider's ears and the sides of his or her head. Basically they cover all the areas of the head on which hair grows. They offer much more protection than half helmets, but they still leave the face exposed. They may save your life should you crash, but they won't save your looks.

### FULL-FACE HELMETS

Half helmets and three-quarter helmets look classic and will save your cranium in an accident, but the chin guard found on a full-faced helmet is what will save your face. These are helmets of the type used by most race car drivers, and with good

**Some people place more importance on seeing what's behind them than do others. You might not need quite as many mirrors as Kent Aldrich to see what's going on back there, but you do need at least a couple.**

Sometimes in organized rallies with many scooters attending you won't have the option of riding in a staggered formation. Make certain your skills are up to snuff before riding in such groups.

reason—they offer the most protection of any helmet, and by a long shot. This is the type of helmet that everyone who rides any sort of motorized two-wheeler should wear.

Many riders of the modern sport-type scooters wear full-faced motocross helmets. These offer full-faced protection but with added ventilation and air flow. The Darth Vader-esque looks of these helmets mixes well with the Star Wars styling of many modern scooters.

Helmet laws vary from state to state, but eyewear is a requirement just about everywhere. Most scooter or motorcycle shops will sell simple clear-framed glasses, but goggles keep out the wind and rain (and look cool to boot). A traditional full-faced helmet will eliminate the need for goggles because the face shield will provide the best eye protection available. If you ride with one of the other types of helmets, including the motocross-style full-face helmet, you will need some form of eye protection.

## RIDING SKILLS

More important than the helmet, though, is that the scooterist is a good rider. As noted in the accompanying sidebar and in the previous chapter, a Motorcycle Safety Foundation course will be the single best way to aquire solid riding skills.

Once you've taken the MSF RiderCourse and learned to ride your scooter properly, ease yourself into real-

## HELMETS TO AVOID

Beware of buying novelty helmets with fake Department of Transportation (DOT) approval stickers. You never want to ride without a DOT-approved helmet, even around the block or to the corner store. Ideally you'll wear a full-face helmet, but the bare minimum helmet you should consider acceptable is a half-helmet with an official DOT approval sticker.

But beware: not all helmets with such stickers are tested and approved by the Department of Transportation. When a number of states passed helmet laws in the early 1990s (many of these have been repealed in the intervening years), a number of motorcyclists began putting fake stickers on plastic novelty helmets (that were little more than toys) as a protest. These helmets certainly didn't pass any recognized testing procedures.

To avoid accidentally buying one of these fake helmets, make certain that the helmet you are buying is properly constructed. The fake helmet will look like a plastic beanie, with little or no Styrofoam cushioning inside the shell. There should be at least an inch of Styrofoam cushioning beneath the plastic or fiberglass outer shell.

Another type of helmet to avoid is an antique "pudding-bowl" style helmet. These are the ancestors of modern half-helmets, and though they were the best helmets available

when originally manufactured, their design is such that they do not offer the minimal acceptable protection by today's standards. Besides, time takes a toll on helmets. The protective foam lining dries out with age and loses its impact-absorbing abilities. A vintage helmet might look wicked cool with your retro-styled scooter, but it will offer no more protection than a fake novelty helmet.

In general, you should avoid used helmets because of the deterioration they suffer with age. Any helmet older than five years should be considered unsafe. If a helmet has suffered even a single impact, it should also be considered unsafe. A helmet is designed to absorb and dissipate the energy from a single impact. After that, all bets are off.

This may seem a bit complicated, but you really only need to remember one thing: if you have any doubts about the quality of the helmet, don't buy it.

world situations. Practice on easy roads before delving into traffic. Learn to ride your scooter in the rain. This is difficult and requires skill, but sooner or later you will be caught in a downpour. It's best to develop the skills before you need them. Get good tires for better traction. Wear gloves and solid boots that cover your ankles. To be extra safe, wear full leathers. Motorcycle shops also sell reinforced riding jackets that can protect you nearly as well as leather.

The first time you ride with a passenger, take it easy and don't show off. The added weight will change the balance of the bike. Don't assume the person on the pillion (the back of the seat) knows how to be a good passenger. Instruct them prior to the ride. Sometimes he or she will shift their weight in the wrong direction, lean too much into the turn, or not hold on tightly.

The dashboard of the TGB 303R Laser sports all the latest gizmos and a speedometer boasting a hopeful 50 mph.

## MOTORCYCLE SAFETY FOUNDATION (MSF) SAVING YOUR NECK

Set up as a not-for-profit organization to save as many lives as possible, the Motorcycle Safety Foundation is a national organization with courses offered in almost every state. While the "motorcycle" moniker may throw off most scooterists, the MSF is sponsored not only by the big motorcycle manufacturers (Harley-Davidson, Honda, and Yamaha) but also by the likes of Piaggio, Ducati, Suzuki, and BMW.

The RiderCourse is a comprehensive class and available for different skill levels. To date, more than one-and-a-half-million motor-cyclists and scooterists have passed the MSF's RiderCourse. Each class covers topics such as managing difficult terrain, proper riding gear, street strategies, effective braking, effective turning, evasive maneuvers, and more.

The goal of the Motorcycle Safety Foundation's RiderCourse is not to make a buck but to help every rider ride safely. A sliding scale offers reduced tuition (some-times even free) to students. Some serious scooter or motorcycle clubs (especially with a brand sponsor) will reimburse course fees as part of their membership package.

The biggest advantage of taking a rider safety course from the Motorcycle Safety Foundation is avoiding a premature funeral, or at least saving yourself from wearing one of those embarrassing foam neck braces.

Other benefits include:

• **Reduced fee or skill test waiver for a motorcycle endorsement on driver's licenses.** Not all states offer this added benefit, but be sure to ask when renewing your license at the DOT.

• **Discounts on insurance.** As part of safe-driver programs, many insurance agents offer a substantial discount on your coverage. With time, the reduced insurance payments will pay for the course.

• **More riding confidence.** Rather than plunging yourself unwittingly into dangerous situations, the MSF's courses show you how to avoid risky traffic.

• **Better car-driving skills.** Not only will the RiderCourse improve your scootering skills, but you'll be more aware behind the wheel.

• **More support for scootering.** As a national organization hooked up with all the major motorcycle and scooter manufacturers, the MSF has long arms to lean on politicians to pass driving laws that better protect scooter-ists and motorcyclists. What's more, through the MSF's programs, scooterists became better riders and therefore not frowned upon so much by motorists in oversized SUVs.

For more information, click on www.msf-usa.org or dial up 1-800-446-9227

## WHAT'S IN THE GIRL'S GLOVE BOX?
### BEK'S ADVICE TO SCOOTER GIRLS

Every scooter magazine or website with a "girly" column includes some kind of "List of What to Pack." Most things you should always carry while scooting are pretty obvious (basic tools, hand wipes, tampons, water, flashlight, cell phone), but here's what other lists miss:

• **Small first aid kit.** Camping stores have ultra-compact lightweight kits with everything you'll need to patch up small spots of road rash and wash up, cover larger wounds, or treat that under-the-helmet bee sting.

• **Your medical insurance information.** Laminate a card with all your emergency contact information and carry it with you at all times! Include family phone numbers, drug allergies (if any), a list of medications you're taking, and a list of any major injuries or surgeries in your history. Make sure it is current. This is a potentially life-saving item that's easy to make at home with a computer, a printer, some cardboard, and clear packing tape.

• **Cheap disposable camera, cocked and loaded.** It can come in handy for unexpected sunsets, or for insurance purposes if you're involved in, or witness, an accident.

• **One large plastic trash bag.** It can be used as an emergency rain poncho, water carrier, ground protectant—or trash bag!

• Duct tape, the greatest temporary fix. In a pinch, it can hold on a side cowl that's snapped its moorings, hold a stack of take-out containers to the seat-back, hold on a mirror just long enough to make it home, hold together broken helmet shields and sun goggles, or hold on corroded, vibrated-apart taillights and turn signals. The most creative scooterists' use of duct tape I've seen (but would not recommend) was used to strap a drunken, passed-out, incoherent friend to the driver for a bumpy ride home.

• **Paper, pencil, and extra lipstick.** You never know!

—Becky Wallace

This stealth Vespa rides under the radar, except that of the police wanting a closer look. *Becky Wallace, owner*

Insist that your passenger wear a helmet, because you're responsible for their safety, as well.

Learn to lean into turns, but look out for slick spots and sand. Don't slam on your brakes on slippery surfaces, but ride it out. Slow down before a turn. Try not to brake while turning, but twist the throttle a bit to speed up around it.

Most states require a motorcycle license to drive a scooter with an engine larger than 50 cc, and many even require a moped license for riding a 50-cc scooter. Many states award a full-fledged motorcycle license to anyone who successfully completes an MSF Basic RiderCourse. In states that don't follow this eminently sensible practice, a rider will have to take a test at the department of motor vehicles. Fortunately, scooterists have a distinct advantage over motorcyclists when taking the driving test. With the low center of gravity over the little wheels, scooters can easily weave through the orange cones and stop on a dime. Even so, practicing at home and seeing the test site beforehand can help ensure a passing grade.

Insurance is the other bureaucratic, but essential, hassle (especially when cops pull you over to break up their boring evenings). Keep your license and tabs up to date to avoid run-ins with the law. Prior to the 1970s, scooters often didn't need to be licensed because they were considered glorified lawnmowers by the cops.

After all the precautions in the world, the biggest danger to scooterists is not Rockers, errant trees, or oil slicks. Bad car drivers are the cause of most fatalities and serious accidents. Never assume a car sees you. (Why do you think the Mods clipped on every light, mirror, and horn they could find?) Drivers eat Big Macs, drink hot coffee, fiddle with the CD player, adjust their GPS, put on mascara, chat on their cell phone, shave, smoke, and fondle their loved ones while behind the wheel. Why should they care about that pesky scooter in the way of their SUV? A scooterist always loses when jousting with an auto. Always. The laws of physics always favor a three-ton motorized behemoth over an unsubstantial vehicle that often weighs less than a filled gas tank on an SUV.

## CARRYING A PASSENGER: KEEPING THE PILLION SAFE

Before giving that certain someone a lift on the back seat, consider these tips to ensure a safe ride and avoid the fuzz or a trip to the emergency room:

• **Accommodating a passenger.** Most states and countries prohibit passengers on scooters of 50 cc or less. Motorcycle/scooter licenses generally allow 16-year-olds (or even 14-year-olds) to drive a moped (scooter) of less than 50 cc without a passenger. Besides, most 50cc scooters are not designed to carry that much weight and you could overwork your engine.

• **Child passengers.** Some states don't allow young passengers, while many countries allow entire families to hop on a single

The digital speedo, tachometer, and odometer on the Grandvista show that this top-of-the-line Kymco is indeed a space-age cruiser. How many other scooters can boast a (working) clock?

The Grandvista stays true to its name by giving the pillion fodder not a bench or saddle seat, but rather an elevated throne. This luxurious tush padding causes the scooter purists to cry foul and dub the Grandvista a Goldwing.

Kymco opted for prestigious telescopic front forks on the 12-inch wheels of the Grandvista for smooth scooting.

scooter. In any case, the parent should give the OK and make sure the helmet is secure and that the child can reach the footrests with both feet.

• **Suspension and tire pressure.** While you should always keep your tires pumped up to the proper pressure as recommended in the owner's manual, this is especially important when a passenger hops on back. Most scooters' suspension is not made for two hefty riders, so double check your owner's manual before giving your chubby buddy a lift.

• **Footrests.** Check to make sure you have either foot pegs jutting out from the rear for the passenger or that the floorboards extend back far enough. Don't assume your passenger knows where to put

Depending on your state laws an engine size of 50cc or smaller may put your vehicle in the "moped" category with this eGO.

The curving vertical front grille of the Kymco People owes a nod to the femininity of the Ford Edsel. Should this be a surprise? After all, scooter visionaries from Corradino d'Ascanio to E. Foster Salsbury always envisioned a woman atop their putt-putts.

his or her feet. Many passengers will extend their legs away from the sidepanels for a tiring and potentially dangerous drive if you like to lean into curves. One of the advantages of most scooters is the covered engine, which helps you avoid burning legs on mufflers or header pipes. If you have exposed hot pipes, make sure you point these out to the pillion passenger.

• **Helmet on your passenger.** Ideally, both driver and passenger should have helmets. This is especially true when you get the occasional "helmet bump" from your passenger during quick stops.

• **Advising your passenger.** The added weight on the back of your scooter radically alters the handling, so help your passenger avoid working against you by intstructing them to lean into the turn. Some passengers, however, can shift their weight so much into the turn that it can be hard to come back up. To avoid touching the rider, many passengers will precariously hold on to the back of their seat or the tire rack behind them. I'd advise the passenger to grab tightly on to your waist (and you can make the excuse that it's far more aerodynamic).

• **Slow cornering.** Give yourself extra room for turning with the extra load on the rear. Beware of sidewinds because you have double the area for the air to push.

• **Riding sidesaddle.** While this makes for a great photo op to imitate those charming Italian babes on the back of a classic Vespa, sidesaddle riding is not safe at any speed.

• **Braking and accelerating slowly.** This may seem obvious, but just make sure you give yourself plenty of room to stop before you end up ramming that Mack truck. Because of the added weight on the rear, you may rely more on the rear brake. Be especially careful braking when going downhill, as the increased weight gives you more propulsion. Don't expect to be able to pass that pokey Ducati as easily as when you ride alone.

## SCOOTER SAFETY: TIPS TO STAY ALIVE

Many scooter riding tips are the same as those drilled into your head at drivers' ed courses. If you were covering your eyes during all those gruesome films, here's a refresher for when you hit the pavement on your new scoot:

• **Assume that motorists can't (or choose not to) see you.** If you imagine that you're invisible, you'll drive much more carefully. Use your horn to prevent a car from bashing you. It's better to have a car driver angry that you honked at them than suffer a five-day stay in the hospital.

Modern scooters vary from vintage to sport scooters. Apart from looks, consider what you need. A 50cc scooter doesn't allow for a passenger, but often doesn't require you taking a motorcycle test either. A heartier 150cc scooter is faster and therefore can get you out of dangerous situations—like away from motorists applying mascara.

Although the Ducati Phantom uses a speedy two-stroke engine, a catalytic exhaust system keeps its pollution (relatively) clean. The racing tires come standard and—with a little adjusting of the governor—encourage youngsters to drag from every stoplight.

• **Never drive in the blind spot.** When riding in traffic, try to make sure that cars and trucks can see you. Adjust your position in the lane to be in their rearview mirror. Even then, don't assume that the driver sees you, even if he or she looks right at you.

• **Keep your headlights on, day or night.** Also, use your turn signals. Scooter turn signals can be hard to see, so once you are comfortable with your riding skills, augment your scooter's turn signals with your own hand signals.

• **Tap brakes to indicate speed change.** If you're decelerating and want to downshift, consider tapping your brake to alert the car behind you.

• **Plop a brightly-colored helmet on your head.** Black helmets are cool but cannot be seen at night. Lighter-colored helmets are a better answer. A strip of reflective tape on your helmet can make you even more visible if driving at night.

• **Wear eye protection.** Imagine your reaction if you got a wasp in your eye while hitting 55 miles per hour on your scooter. Scooter shops even sell cool, clear, non-prescription glasses to protect your eyes at night.

• **If driving at night, tape on reflective strips around your scooter.** Wearing a Velcro reflective band on your leg could save your life.

• **Don't drive tired or drunk.** Wait until you're done scooting around to have a beer or guzzle cough syrup.

• **Don't talk on your cell phone while driving (unless you're Italian).** Only bona fide Italians are permitted to smoke a cigarette and chat on their cell phones while shifting their Vespa through traffic.

• **Anticipate danger.** Watch the road ahead and imagine different scenarios. Don't expect car drivers to politely put on their turn signal. Give yourself space to swerve around potholes or to avoid braking over oil slicks and sand traps.

• **Wear appropriate clothing.** Flip-flops and shorts lead to vicious raspberries. While zooming around the Amalfi Coast in 95-degree weather may seem like a call for bikinis and espadrilles, sliding on sand at 40 miles per hour will make that sunburn seem pleasant. Long pants, boots, and gloves (especially leather) are your only protection against the asphalt.

• **Sign up for the Motorcycle Safety Foundation RiderCourse.** Go to www.msf-usa.org or dial up 1-800-446-9227. See the MSF sidebar for more information.

When passengers hop on the rear seat, make sure they hold you tightly around the waist and put their feet firmly on the rear pegs.

• **Practice makes perfect.** Before risking rush-hour traffic or, God forbid, the interstate, tool around side streets and parking lots. Go fast, go slow, brake fast, downshift, learn to lean into turns. Remember learning how to drive on ice by doing donuts in an empty parking lot? Practice tooling in circles (not on ice!) with no dangerous drivers to trip you up.

• **Find the horn and signals.** Before you set off on the streets, locate your turn signals and horn so you can warn other drivers about your intentions.

• **Keep at least two seconds of space between you and the car in front of you.** Find a telephone pole on the side of the road as a landmark. When the car in front of you passes it, count "one-one thousand, two-one thousand," at which time you should pass the pole. For extra safe driving, allow one second per 10 miles per hour. For example, if you're driving 40 miles per hour, allow a four second count.

## TOUGH TERRAIN: NEWTON CAN SAVE YOUR NECK

Apply geometry and Newtonian laws of motion to your putt-putt. When you see difficult terrain ahead, slow down and downshift before you hit it. Remember Newton's first law: an object in motion tends to stay in motion with the same speed and in the same direction. So just keep it nice and steady over the problem spot.

When crossing railroad tracks, keep your wheels perpendicular to the rails to prevent your tires from getting stuck in the ruts. Over any rough surface, try to stay straight and avoid turning or changing speed dramatically. Grip the handlebars firmly, but don't tense up your arms and body. Allow your body to be a giant shock absorber that moves easily over the bumps.

If you have to go over a large hump, like a railroad track or wooden board, lean back before you hit it and then forward once the first wheel is over it. This way you

The space-age dual dashboard of the Piaggio X9 may seem a distraction at first, but once on the road it's nice to be aware every aspect of your scooter's performance—all in a sleek Italian design of digital and dials.

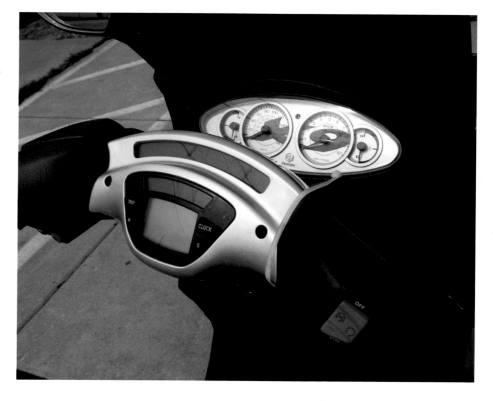

Before twisting the throttle and risking traffic, get acquainted with all the bells and whistles of your scooter. Turn signals on scooters usually don't turn off after completing the turn, so remember to switch them off to avoid unpleasantries with hurried motorists.

Two-cylinders fire inside the 650 Burgman engine, the largest scooter so far conceived with a big price tag of $12,990 to boot. The 525 pounds are halted thanks to a 230mm rear disc brake.

lessen the load on the wheel that needs to pop over the bump.

If your tire blows out, immediately back off the throttle (and pull in the clutch if you have a manual transmission). Keep your bike straight. The shattered tire will probably decelerate you in due time, but you can apply a bit of brake to slow down gradually.

While Newtonian physics can help you stay safe, accidents, on the other hand, are more easily explained by vector or chaos theory.

## INSURANCE AND LICENSING: JUMPING BUREAUCRATIC HURDLES

Most states require a separate motorcycle endorsement on your driver's license to allow you to legally operate a scooter. Some states

don't know how to list a scooter (is it a moped or a motorcycle?), so they will sometimes let you avoid taking the motorcycle test if your bike is less than 50 or 100 cc. Even so, both the written and riding motorcycle test will help ensure that you are a competent scooter driver. Each state varies in their requirements, so contact your local department of motor vehicles for information.

Some states will grant you a motorcycle endorsement when you complete a MSF Basic RiderCourse. This is the very best (and also the easiest) way to get a motorcycle endorsement. It's the easiest way because you will have trained professionals coaching you through the process. It's the best and safest way because it ensures that you not only have an endorsement to operate your scooter, but you also have the skills to do so safely. If your state allows you to receive an endorsement in this manner, you would be well advised to do so.

When you register your scooter, the department of motor vehicles usually asks for your insurance policy number. But how can you have insurance on a bike that isn't registered? This chicken-and-egg dilemma isn't as much of a Catch-22 as you'd think. If you have an existing motor-vehicle insurance policy, you simply contact your insurance agent prior to purchasing the scooter and inform him or her about your intentions. If you have a decent relationship with the agent, he or she will just ask you to phone in the appropriate information once the transaction is completed. Then you just supply your existing policy number when you register the scooter.

In fact, most often you won't register the scooter yourself. If you buy a brand new scooter from a dealer, in most states the dealer will register the scooter and include all tax and licensing fees in the price of the scooter.

If you buy a used scooter from a private party, it gets a bit more complicated. Then you will have to register the scooter yourself. Again, your first step needs to be contacting your insurance agent and letting him or her know you are buying a scooter. After that you will need to go to your appropriate state licensing department and register the scooter yourself. If you do this prior to receiving a policy number from your insurance agent, in most locales this won't be a problem. Usually the department of motor vehicles will give you a grace period to call in your information, and in the meantime they just ask for the insurance company.

What if you don't have an insurance agent? Get one. Shop around for insurance before settling on one company. Your best bet is your homeowner's insurance company, if you own a home. Your next best bet is often the same company that insures your automobile. Usually such companies will provide excellent rates for multi-vehicle policies, but not always. While the company that insures your home or car may well be your best bet, you may find better deals elsewhere, or you may even find your company does not insure motorcycles or scooters.

Many agencies will raise rates solely based on where you live; others won't even insure scooters at all. Some companies won't insure a rider based on his or her credit rating, or the rates such companies offer may be much higher for someone with a bad credit rating. Because insurance agents generally know little about mopeds, scooters, and motorcycles, rates rise according to engine size. Scooterists benefit because of the relatively small engines under their bodywork.

Most states require that you have liability insurance at the very least. Comprehensive and collision policies are available for more cash out of your pocket. The uninsured driver policy is handy in case a poor drunk with no coverage clips you from the side. If you have comprehensive coverage and want to reduce your annual premiums ask about getting a larger deductible on your policy. Don't forget to ask about discounts for nonsmokers, married status, good-student record, perfect

Modern scooters offer a relatively spacious glovebox to stash your tool kit, helmet, or other contraband.

driving record, etc. Ask your insurance agent if they'll give you a discount if you've completed the Motorcycle Safety Foundation's RiderCourse.

If you do go for a more expensive comprehensive policy, be careful about filing claims. It might seem great to collect a check

While Suzuki's 650 Burgman may be the most expensive and most powerful scooter ever, the continuously variable transmission (CVT) is an updated version of the 1930's-era Salsbury and Moto-Scoot designs.

As the saying goes, "You can always judge a happy scooterists by the bugs on their teeth." In spite of its less-than-aerodynamic design, the Yamaha Zuma was a surprise success in the scooter world because of its high performance and easy handling.

for $500 after your scooter falls over in a parking lot, but you might end up paying a lot more than that in the long run. Although it's always great to collect insurance money for the smallest little ding on the sidepanel, the insurance company will always get their money back by raising their rates.

## START SEEING SCOOTERS! BEING A RESPECTFUL MOTORIST

Most of the tips in this book focus on being a better scooterist, but the most dangerous situations are created by car drivers. You can minimize the danger of a single-vehicle accident by developing proper skills and wearing proper gear, but safety gear can only do so much to protect you when the decaf-nonfat-latte-swilling, cell-phone-yakking, baby-spittle-wiping driver gets distracted and runs you down with three tons of SUV. As you become a more experienced scooterist, you will develop skills and techniques to help avoid such drivers. (*How to Ride a Motorcycle* and *Ride Hard, Ride Smart*, both by Pat Hahn and available from Motorbooks.com, are filled with such tips and techniques.) To some degree, however, you will always be at the mercy of the larger vehicles on the road.

Help your car-dependent friends and relatives to be the best drivers they can be and avoid having your scooter friends wiped from their windshields. And practice what you preach; most scooterists have to resort to an automobile when the snow begins to fly or that thunderstorm strikes.

Here are some tips for being a more scooter-friendly driver; practice them when you're driving your car and share them with your car-driving friends.

• **Give scooters plenty of room.** Nothing makes a scooterist more nervous (and more likely to do something stupid) than an eager automobile on his or her tail. Because I often downshift to slow down, my brake light doesn't turn on and a tail-gating car won't stop in time. Classic scooters use a magneto rather than a battery and tend to have very dim brake lights, and they're only brightened when the motor is revved, which won't be happening when the scooter is decelerating.

• **Give scooters a lane.** Don't treat a scooter like a bicycle that should ride snug to the curb. If scooters swerve around within their lane, don't assume they're showing off how agile the little putt-putt is. Scooterists will often swerve around within their lane to avoid potholes, manhole covers, sand traps, or patches of oil.

• **Check your blind spot.** Most vehicles have blind spots big enough to disguise a large SUV; imagine how easily a scooter can be overlooked. Make sure your mirrors are properly adjusted to minimize your blind spot. Hint: your sideview mirrors are called "sideview mirrors" because they are designed to show you what's beside you. The rearview mirror is designed to show you what's behind you. Unfortunately, most drivers adjust their sideview mirrors to show them the rear view. Many people learned this improper technique in drivers' ed class. If you adjust your mirrors so that you can see the rear corners of your car, you are using this improper method. Think about it: is it more important to see the rear corner of your car or the vehicles driving in your blind spot?

Even when your mirrors are properly adjusted, your vehicle will still most likely have a blind spot big enough to hide a scooter. If your mirrors are properly adjusted, you'll be able to see most of the blind spot by simply glancing to the side without turning your head. Before swerving out, take a second to double check for any Vespas on the horizon.

You still can't be 100 percent certain you've seen everything there is to see once you've committed to changing lanes. A great method for safely changing lanes without creaming a scooter (or car or SUV) you failed to see is to practice what Pat Hahn calls the "soft lane change" in his books *Ride Hard, Ride Smart* and *How to Ride a Motorcycle*. Using the soft lane change means that once you've cleared the lane visually, you turn on your signal and slowly ease into the next lane instead of darting into the lane like a highly-caffeinated lab rat. This will let all other drivers know your intentions, and give any vehicle you might have visually missed a chance to move to a safety zone while you change lanes.

The soft lane change is a good technique to use on your scooter as well. Believe it or not, you will have a fairly large blind spot in your scooter mirrors. Unfortunately your scooter mirrors have to serve as both sideview and rearview mirrors, since you won't have the large rearview mirror found on a car.

Another way to help other drivers see you is to avoid riding in a car's blind spot. If you ride where other drivers can see you, either in front of them or far enough behind them so that you can see their face in the sideview mirror, there is at least the possibility that the other drivers will see you. You should always assume that the other drivers don't see you, but if you ride in a blind spot you guarantee they won't.

• **Be careful of those turn signals.** Many drivers have never grasped the concept of the turn signal, simple as that may be, judging by the astounding number

With a Chianti-red paint scheme and a name like "Vino," Yamaha's vintage-styled scooter tempts riders to tip back some of that red, red wine and go for a joy ride. Remember the scooter axiom, though, "Lambrusco and Lambrettas do not mix."

Part scooter, part ape hanger. The Vino 125 has classic lines reminiscent of the early Vespas—in fact its ads hop on the Fellini bandwagon with claims of "La Dolce Vita." The handlebars, however, seem like they've been borrowed off a Harley hog. Can Paparazzo still keep one hand on the grip and the other shooting Anita Ekberg in the Fontana di Trevi?

of people who don't signal their lane changes. Don't be one of them. Always signal your turns and lane changes; that way you at least give scooter riders a chance to get out of your way if you fail to see them prior to changing lanes.

You also need to pay special attention to scooters making turns. Even on modern scooters (especially those from a particular boot-shaped country) the electrical system is so weak that the turn signals can be very difficult to see in broad daylight. This is why it's a good idea for scooter riders to augment their electric turn signals with hand signals.

You also want to watch for scooters with turn signals flashing even when they aren't making a turn. Scooter turn signals don't cancel themselves after turning, and many scooterists forget to turn them off. (At least they're signaling, unlike many deviant drivers.) When you're riding your scooter, make a habit of pushing the "cancel" button on the turn signals every now and then to

make certain you're not riding down the street with your turn signals flashing.

- **Don't honk.** Some motorists feel they are just letting the scooterist know they are behind them by tailgating them and giving a polite little toot of the horn. After much harassment, most scooterists assume that car drivers want them off the road anyway. I've been startled to the point of almost going off the road, and then had the driver give an enthusiastic wave as my heart is pounding from the near accident. Please, don't beep, just wave.

- **Realize a scooter may be closer than it seems.** Because scooters only have one headlight (except for Zumas, which have two headlights that are so dim they can hardly be seen unless the engine is revving towards redline), judging their speed and distance can be tricky at night. Assume the scooter is closer than it appears.

- **Don't hate scooters.** Many drivers view scooters, bicycles, mopeds, and motorcycles as a nuisance that stands in the way of their trip to the strip mall. Drive a scooter and you'll not only be impressed at how incredibly fun they are, but also by how vulnerable they are. Give that scooter space because that could be your friend or relative atop those two wheels.

- **Remember that cars win.** In a collision with a scooter, cars will usually only suffer a scratch or an unseemly dent. The scooterist ends up in the hospital. Picture the scooterist as an unshielded person flying by rather than another metal box with a big bumper.

## EMERGENCY MANEUVERS: DAMN CABLES BROKE AGAIN

Most stock modern scooters are relatively trouble free (with the exception of Italian electrical systems, but that is a book in itself). Most mechanical problems arise when the owner starts modifying the scooter. Vintage scooters are the polar opposite. Whatever can go wrong on a vintage scooter likely will go wrong. Sometimes they can be dangerous.

Two nightmare situations can arise via malevolent cables, but they have simple solutions if you are prepared. Both can also happen on a modern scooter (though the snapped clutch cable can only happen on one of the handful of modern scooters with manual transmissions), so it would be

## PILLION FODDER? BEK'S ADVICE IF YOU RIDE BEHIND

If you find yourself in a situation where you must ride on the back ("bitch" or "cupcake," depending on the gender), keep in mind:

1. Lean with the driver, not against him/her.
2. Hang onto the driver with both hands, not onto the back of the seat.
3. Don't lean at crazy angles to take photos, point at scenery, cop a feel, or check yourself out in shop windows.
4. Don't yell or scream in the driver's ear, no matter how scared or excited you are.
5. Keep your feet on the floorboards at all times, even at stops.
6. Don't step on the kick-start lever.
7. Always remember to say "thank you!"
   —Becky Wallace

Dual saddle seats on this Lambretta LD look classic but would any passenger actually hold on to only the little handle in front of the rear seat? For maximum safety, the pillion passenger should hold on tightly to the waist of the driver.

wise for even a modern scooter owner to be prepared.

• **Snapped clutch cable.** If you're tooling along at full speed and try to downshift, what do you do if you pull the clutch lever and it just dangles limply? The clutch doesn't pop back and you don't seem to be able to shift. Your clutch cable is kaput, but don't panic. Stop giving the engine so much gas and forceably twist the left handle grip into the next lower gear. You can shift without a clutch, although it can be a bit jumpy. Try to twist the shifter into neutral and then brake to a

Rather than opting for the digital read-out displays on many of the modern scooters, Yamaha chose the more legible dials for its 400cc Majesty maxi-scooter. Besides, isn't it more fun to rev a scooter with a little red hand that flicks wildly to the right on the speedometer?

stop. You have spare cables in the glove box, right? Of course, this scenario is only relevant if you have a geared scooter.

• **Throttle is stuck wide open.** This can happen to any scooter, even a brand new Japanese model. Imagine that you're zooming along happily and the throttle doesn't twist back like it's supposed to. The throttle cable is stuck open. First twist hard to try to push the cable through. Hit the cut-off switch (you found out where it is when you took the MSF course, right?). Pull in the clutch, put the scooter in neutral and brake to a stop.

The front brakes on the Vino 125 are an ample 180 mm disc to stop its 229 pound from zooming along.

## RALLY RIDING:
## TIPS FOR SCOOTER FORMATION

You may feel like you've mastered your scooter after taking your MSF RiderCourse, but don't assume that riding in that snappy group of scooters is as easy as it looks. Here's some advice before starting your snake of scooters:

• **Ride staggered or single file.** While side-by-side looks the best in any parade, this formation is recommended only at slow speeds or when waiting at a stoplight. If a pothole presents itself, you have less room to swerve if a fellow scooterist is on one side and

What better way to be seen while scooting along than attaching slick chrome wheel covers? This new Vespa carries on the Mod tradition of miles of chrome and two-tone paint schemes.

the curb on the other. Staggered scooters are the safest bet at cruising speed, and single file is mandatory around curves.

• **Consider small vs. large group.** Small groups are easiest to manage, but a huge line of scooters weaving through downtown will inevitably impress voyeurs (though may arouse the interest of the local police department). The downside is running red lights to keep up with the pack and a few show-offs who can't resist revving their newly bored-out engine.

• **Pump up.** Stopping a whole line of scooters because you forgot to fill up will inevitably annoy your friends. Fill 'er up before getting in line.

• **Take maps.** Although nerdy, maps and route directions can keep the scooter snake flowing with ease.

• **Assign a leader and a caboose.** Having two leaders with slightly different ideas of the route can lead to moving discussions and a much-welcomed coup d'état. As history has taught us, dictatorships lead with deadly efficiency. A sweep, or tail rider, can pick up any stragglers to keep them marching in step.

• **Remember cell phone and tool kit.** At least one person in the pack should carry cables, tools, a cell phone, and a first aid kit. For longer trips of vintage bikes, consider having a scooter-less friend driving a pickup truck to carry the inevitable broken down scooters.

When I traveled to the Piaggio factory in Pontedera (near Pisa) in the 1990s, I was told my Italian hosts, "Every designer wants his hands on the new Vespa. They all want to be able to sign their name to it." This attention to Italian design is clear in every aspect of the new Vespa.

# MINIMUM MAINTENANCE

## RULES FOR PACKING

- Ten steps to keep your scooter tuned to perfection
- How to avoid being a victim of scooter thievery
- Everything you'll need in your glovebox when the damn scooter stalls
- When to clean or toss your spark plugs
- How to change your oil before the engine seizes
- Modifying your putt-putt for maximum rpms

*Vespa mit seitenwagen*

**While scooters with side cars may seem like a match, the early Vespas struggled with heaving the new heft up any sort of hill, especially along the switchbacks of the Rhine valley where this beauty lives.**

All too often scooterists are stigmatized by the fact that they've never even looked under the side panels until the bike is broken. Read *Zen and the Art of Motorcycle Maintenance* to realize that the rider must be one with his or her ride, and to do that you must understand everything about it. Buy the repair manual for your scooter and start with some very basic updates. Pull out the ratchet and screwdriver and take things apart for fun. The beauty of older scooters is their simplicity. Consider it an ingenious puzzle and you have the answer key, thanks to your repair manual.

### WHAT'S IN THE GLOVE BOX? SCOOTER TOOL KIT FOR THE MECHANICALLY UNINCLINED

In the 1950s, both Piaggio and Innocenti marketed the idea of "trouble-free scootering" with their service shops around Europe to help scooterists in need.

Innocenti upped the ante against Piaggio by forming the "Blue Angels," a sort of scooter AAA that would zoom out to help broken down Lambrettas.

Many scooter riders, on the other hand, knew how temperamental their zippy two-strokes could be and scoffed at the idea of "trouble-free scootering." They valued a rider's ability to maintain his or her own scooter, and to this day this ability retains a good deal of value.

Motorscooter maintenance is a form of meditation in which you discover how your vehicle—and yourself, by default—function and fit into this world. Any scooter club will recommend you stuff your glove box full of helpful tools and ignore the optimist who says you'll have no problems.

After years of pushing my Lambretta Li 125 Slimline as much as I rode it, I offer my advice and recommend you keep these tools in the glove box:

• **Socket wrench, rag, and wire brush**. This is especially important when riding a two-stroke, old or new; not only does that smokey blue exhaust pollute the air, but it also pollutes the engine's combustion chamber. No matter how careful you are about mixing the proper ratio of oil to gas, sooner or later your spark plug will become fouled with carbon. When this becomes severe enough, eventually your scooter won't start. When the damn Lammie won't fire, I pull the plug and wipe off the soot from the tip. As a last resort, I use a wire brush to clean it, but this will wear down the plug.

• **Spark plug gapper**. Checking and setting the gap for the spark plug is essential for smooth scooting, especially after you've cleaned the tip of the spark plug with a wire

A look under the vintage-looking exterior of the Venice reveals all the amenities of modern putt-putts. The minimum maintenance of new scooters allows the mechanically uninclined to avoid the joys of being elbow-deep in grease.

The rotund rump of the **TN'G Milano** avoids the squared-off look begun in the '70s with Lambretta and harkens back to the gay days of *Roman Holiday*.

## SAFETY CHECK: 10 STEPS TO A WELL-TUNED SCOOTER

Before you zoom off on your scooter, check a few mechanical parts each time:

• **Brakes.** Especially if rain poured the night before, brake pads (or discs) can be a bit slippery and will not stop you as quickly as usual.

• **Headlamp, rear light, brake light, turn signals** (if applicable). Older scooters tend to shake and rattle all the connections loose. Better to know immediately that your taillight is broken (or dim) before drivers begin swearing at you.

• **Tire pressure.** No rider is going to pull out the air pressure gauge each time he or she rides, but at the very least glance and see if the tire looks low or the rubber cracked. You should check air pressure if the scooter has sat for several days without being ridden, however. Low pressure can cause unstable handling. High pressure or a damaged tire can cause a blow out—but could provide a spectacular stunt show for nearby drivers. Proper tire care is a critical part of surviving your scooter, and will be discussed in more detail below.

• **Gas/petrol and oil.** Look for the telltale oil spot under your scooter—the early Italian scoots seem especially leaky—and avoid lighting a cigarette unless a two-wheeled Molotov cocktail would impress your buddies.

• **Idiot lights.** If you have a modern scooter with warning lights, heed those immediately. Unfortunately by the time the light blinks, the problem is often serious.

Every 1,000 to 3,000 miles, or at the beginning of the summer, check the following:

• **Screws, nuts, and bolts.** Once the rubber wears down and your whole scooter shakes with the sweet vibrations of the engine, all the attachments will slowly loosen themselves. Pull out the ratchet, wrench, and screwdriver and give them an extra turn (but be careful not to overtighten and strip bolts).

• **Air filter.** Sometimes the filter can just be shaken out, but a new one will help avoid bad stuff entering the engine.

• **Brake pads, discs, and/or fluid (if applicable).** Check your handy-dandy repair manual for the specifications.

• **Cables.** Lubricate your brake, clutch, and gear cables with a bit of grease and they'll work much more smoothly.

• **Engine oil, filter, and transmission fluid (if applicable).** If you go by the theory, "If it's not broken, don't fix it," remember that it has to be in bad condition to break. Don't forget the other adage, "An ounce of prevention is worth a pound of cure."

• **Swiss army knife, pliers, and crescent wrench**. Sure, you *should* bring all sorts of proper wrenches and screwdrivers, but you won't have room. Pliers will eventually strip nuts and bolts, as will adjustable wrenches like a crescent wrench, but you won't care when you're stuck on the side of the road.

• **Plastic measuring cup and a little funnel**. This only applies to vintage scooters, since all modern two-stroke scooters automatically mix gas and oil. If you ride one of the antiques, you'll need to make certain your tank contains the proper ratio of oil to gas. Look in your repair manual for the proper mix. If you have too much oil, the scooter will have trouble starting and the plug could foul up. If you don't have enough, the engine will burn hot and could seize. Some gas stations have paper funnels so you don't spill gas all over your ride. If you're fastidious, though, bring your own funnel. Spilled gas cracks paint.

brush. Simply pull off the plug with the socket wrench, and slip the gapper in the end to get the correct measurement (as shown in your repair manual).

• **Repair manual**. Unsympathetic publishers print oversized books that don't fit in the glove box. Either editors haven't been stranded on a date with a broken down scooter or they can afford to pay a mechanic to tune their ride (usually a motorcycle) perfectly.

• **Extra cable and Allen wrenches**. Nothing stops a rally like a snapped cable. Make sure the spare cable is long enough for every application (in a pinch, tandem bike cables might work). Lambrettas require an Allen wrench to tighten the gear shifting cables (an excruciating task).

Most states allow vintage scooters to have a coveted classic license plate. Technically, this only allows driving to and from rallies and the occasional joy ride around the lakes. Insurance rates generally drop with classic plates as well.

## LOCKED OUT:
### KEYS, CABLES, AND KRYPTONITE

• **Get duplicate keys for the scooter.** Usually locksmiths will have no blanks for scooter keys (especially older ones), so consult your local scooter shop.

• **Don't rely on old scooter locks.** Only a handful of different keys were used on early bikes, which is why Jimmy Cooper in *Quadrophenia* could so easily swipe Sting's scooter and run it off a cliff.

These Vespas await a tune-up at Scooterville in Minneapolis. Owning a vintage scooter either requires a mechanically-inclined owner or a close friendship with a mechanic.

Keeping the spit-shine to the plastic may not lower wind resistance, but it sure makes a Ducati look faster.

Early Vespas all shared keys that were
virtually interchangeable, making scooter
theft a fairly common phenomenon.
Nowadays, Vespa keys have cast off their
rudimentary "theft-proof" technology and
actually keep the scooter safe by using
computer chip technology. That is, if the
crooks don't just pop the whole thing in
their pick-up.

*"The mirrors and the
chromium of the 'classic' mod
scooter reflected not only the
group aspirations of the Mods
but a whole historical
Imaginary, the Imaginary of
affluence. The perfection of
surfaces within Mod was part
of the general 'aestheticization'
of everyday life…"*
—Dick Hebdige

• **Any lock can be cut given enough time.** Most bandits, however, will leave your scoot alone if a chunky kryptonite lock secures it. The downside is carrying a weighty lock that often doesn't fit in your glove box.

• **Run the cable or chain through the wheel**. Make sure, though, that crafty crooks can't just loosen the axle bolt and pop off the lock.

• **Fasten your Kryptonite lock to a post, bike rack, or other immovable object.** Otherwise scooter thieves can just pop your beloved ride in their trunk. If parking en masse, scooters can be locked together.

• **Use a brightly-colored lock.** Bright blaze-orange locks are ugly but show thieves that your scooter is secure before

they start breaking the column lock. They can also help you remember to remove the lock from your brake disc before you ride off and lock up your wheel.

• **Park inside.** Staying at hotels and living in apartments are not conducive to parking your scooter inside because full tanks of gas can bring the building down with a boom. Ask if you can sneak your scoot into the garage or at least park it in full view of a security camera.

• **Consider adding an alarm.** If you must park your scooter in a questionable area at night (and your ride is valuable), mount an alarm that can hook up to your battery. Sure, crooks can still swipe it, but someone may notice.

Rather than using all high-tech digital dials, the updated Vespa dashboard harkens back to the beautiful clam-shell of the classic round body scooters of yore.

• **Wedge your scooter back into your garage.** Park your car after your scooter, so any sly scooter thief will have to steal the car as well, or carry your ride over the roof. If that's not possible, at least make the thief haul out the shovel and lawnmower if they really want your scooter.

• **Lock the column lock, ignition lock, and any other locks each time you park.** Put the key in your pocket.

• **Don't rely on column locks.** Use the locks built into your scooter, but don't rely on them. Although locking the handlebars to the side will deter kids from hopping on

your ride, jamming the handlebars straight with enough force can break the little piece of metal that locks your bike.

• **Keep insurance cards in your wallet or purse.** Your insurance and bike registration shouldn't be kept in the glove box (as convenient as that may be) but on your person. This way, you can more easily contact the police if they swipe your bike. The title for your scooter always stays at home.

• **Customize your scooter.** Who needs the factory finish when you can have an artsy scooter of your own. If you still want it slick and stock, add some smaller

The 200cc engine of the Vespa Granturismo puts the old P200 series in the dust. The four-stroke sits atop 12-inch tires to easily zip around motorists yakking into their cell phones who are too busy to notice that pesky scooter in the way of their SUV.

## A MUST-HAVE TOOL KIT BY STEPHEN HELLER

- **Spark plug**: If fouled, you're stuck. It's small and easy to carry.
- **Spark plug wrench**: Spare plug is useless without it.
- **Clutch cable**: Voted most likely to break on a geared scooter.
- **Gear cable:** Second most likely to snap on a geared scooter.
- **Two-stroke oil**: No oil equals seized engine. No tool will help you then.
- **Tire tube/repair kit:** When you're flat and out of air.
- **Electrical tape:** Wires wiggle loose; put them back together.

- **Needle-nose pliers:** To grip things.
- **Slotted and Phillips screwdrivers:** To screw things that are loose.
- **Wrenches:** Bring the size for the most common nuts and bolt on your bike—rims, seat bucket, etc.
- **Rain gear:** It's nice to be dry.
- **Cable lock:** I trust you, just not the guy behind you.
- **Extra helmet and/or eye protection:** Hey lady, do you want a ride?
- **Flashlight:** Now where did I put that?
- **Pen and paper:** Did you catch that guy's license plate?

markings or unique traits to your bike so you can recognize it in the pack. Don't forget to take photos of your scooter!

### FOIL THE THIEVES: SIMPLE TIPS TO PROTECT SCOOTERS

Apart from the obvious techniques to protect your bike from organized scooter crime, here are a few little tips:

- **Leave your scooter in gear (if it's manual).** Most thieves will deduce that the handlebar levers are for braking (like a bicycle) and wouldn't dream that you have to hold in the clutch lever and twist to put the scooter in neutral.

- **Turn off the fuel petcock and the choke.** The following applies to vintage scooters, especially shutting off the fuel petcock, since most modern scooters don't have easily accessible fuel petcocks. Most thieves don't know a thing about starting a scooter and many won't start without being choked. When you shut off the petcock, the only fuel available to the engine will be that found in the fuel line and the carburetor float bowl (no fuel-injected scooter will have an easily accessible fuel petcock). The few drops of gas in the line will allow the crook to go only a couple of blocks before stalling.

- **Cover your scooter.** Not only does this protect your ride from the elements, but most thieves won't bother ripping off the cover to see what's underneath. Some covers can even be locked.

- **Add an on-off switch in the locked glove box.** Find the electrical wires from the battery or magneto, run it into the glove box, and splice in a toggle switch (or even a doorbell sans chimes). Most thieves aren't too bright and wouldn't figure out this jury-rigged scooter.

To dispel that sinking feeling of quick braking on a Vespa, Piaggio updated the Granturismo brakes to 220mm hydraulic disc on its larger 12-inch wheels.

How many scooters can boast the option of ABS anti-lock brakes on the wheels? Enter: Honda's Silver Wing. With a 582cc engine, being able to stop this beast is a must.

Tucked under the side panels and plastic bodywork lies one of the largest motors ever plunked on a scooter. This 582cc powerplant on Honda's Silver Wing raises the question: Can size excel a scooter right out of being classified a scooter?

When Honda released the 250cc Helix in the 1980s, the scooter faithful cried "foul!" This two-wheeled La-Z-Boy zoomed passed all the competition and Honda didn't heed the critics. Even the keeper of the Lambretta flame, Vittorio Tessera, sprung for a Helix and declared in 1997, "Now that's a scooter!" Always in search of updates, Honda released the Silver Wing as the ultimate maxiscooter with double the engine of the Helix.

## MISSING PUTT-PUTT: WHEN YOUR SCOOTER IS STOLEN

My Lambretta was stolen three times and each time I got it back. Here's how:

• **Report the theft to Officer Friendly.** (Remember: cops hate scooters.) When I asked one of our cities' finest what they're going to do to get my Lammie back, he replied, "Oh, if someone turns it in, we'll call you up." In other words, if the scooter thief has a guilty conscience and can't live with his despicable deed, I'll see my scooter again. "Yup, that's about it," the policeman replied.

• **Customize your scooter, write down the serial number, and take a picture of your scooter.** Of course, you should do these things before your scooter is gone. These will help identify your scooter when (or if) you see it again. Sometimes macho thieves will claim this bike belongs to them and you need proof. Use the photo of your scooter to ask people if they've seen it. Remember that "scooter" can mean everything from handicap wheelchair to child's push toy.

•**Scour the alleys immediately.** Chances are your scooter is still within a five-block area of where you left it, especially if they haven't figured out how to turn on the gas supply. Hop on your bicycle and begin looking.

Two out of the three thefts of my scooter, I found my poor Lammie abandoned because only I could understand exactly how to make it purr. The other time, the police found my stolen scooter. (Our tax dollars at work!) Of course, they did make

me pay to get it out of the impound lot after the thieves abandoned it.

## WINTER STORAGE: PULL THE BATTERY

Living in cold climes calls for stashing the scooter behind the snowblower for long, dark months. If you have a battery on your bike, pull it off and store it somewhere relatively warm or else charge it with a trickle charger over the winter.

## BREAKING IN: READY, STEADY. . . SLOW!

Imagine having a brand new scooter or a vintage scooter with a newly tricked-out engine ready to be driven. After months or even years of waiting for that dream scooter, the urge to blast down the highway at top speed is almost irrepressible. After all, don't you want to know how fast your ride is?

Unfortunately, breaking in a new engine requires sedate riding at—ho-hum—

The distinctive dual headlamps of Yamaha's Zuma not only scare off errant cats but make Zuma-spotting a cinch.

The single-shock on the telescopic forks of Yamaha's Zuma is accompanied by a slick 155mm disc brake.

medium speeds. Follow the manufacturer's recommended break-in procedure, which usually suggests calm, practical driving for the first hundred miles (at least) and not topping out the rpm just to wake the neighborhood. If you're new to scooterdom, this is wise advice to get a feel for how your scooter handles in unexpected situations. By the time you can blast the carbon out of the piston, the initial excitement is gone. Alas, this is the conundrum of speed!

The break-in procedure will differ between a two-stroke and a four-stroke engine, and may vary from manufacturer to manufacturer. While some methods may be better than others, following the one recommended by the scooter's manufacturer will be best should any warranty work be required.

## DEAD MOTOR? STARTING A RELUCTANT SCOOTER

If your engine seems dead, some of these things to check may seem obvious, but just hope you're troubles are this simple. Here's a checklist of possible problems:

## IT'S A GIRL'S, GIRL'S, GIRL'S, GIRL'S WORLD:
### BEK'S ADVICE TO SCOOTER GIRLS

• **Riding in skirts and dresses.** Never an impossibility, always a bad idea. Riding without long pants and a jacket is never a good idea. In the summer, when temperatures rise, you can get these items in mesh material for greater comfort.

• **Owning a scooter.** You aren't really a true scooter girl until you actually own and ride your own. Scooter girls are not "girlfriends of scooter guys," scooter-rally groupies, female "scooter enthusiasts," girls who take a lot of pictures of scooters, or perpetual borrowers of other people's scooters (unless yours is rightfully broken down). That registration card should proudly bear your name, even if it was a gift from Mr. Right.

• **On helmets and hair.** One of the most critical areas of scootergirlship! If you wear a helmet by choice or by law and have a carefully tended hairdo, always pack a comb and tiny bottle of hair spray to revive your style. This is the second-most important use for rear-view mirrors. If you take your bucket off and it's looking pretty hopeless, use every-girl backup items like clips, bobby pins, headbands, and ponytail holders. Pack these into a plastic bag and toss it in your glove box so they're always handy and protected from oil and grime. Long hair and helmets? Believe it or not, braiding it can be one of the best ways to keep it out of your grill and at bay for a long ride. You may look like Heidi, but at least it won't be whipping around wildly or a tangled bird's nest to deal with when you arrive. Also beware of bulky "scrunchies" holding your hair at the base of your neck—it can interfere with the range of motion of your head when wearing a helmet. Consider a frizzy perm and a pick that matches the color of your scooter for the easiest management and highest style.

• **Stinky scooter boys and you.** Unfortunately, girls can't escape the battle of the sexes, even when everyone is on the level playing field of riding scooters. Many scooter boys will be boys. There are rare exceptions, but be prepared for them to underestimate your riding ability, ridicule your mechanical aptitude, doubt your courage and strength, or at the very least, try to get into your pants. Every girl is different, but all girls look silly trying to "overcompensate." You have nothing to prove, and don't need to be "one of the guys" to fit in. Enjoy riding, enjoy flattery, and enjoy being a scooter girl.

—Becky Wallace

• **Gas.** Make sure you have enough in the tank and that the petcock is on (if your scooter is equipped with a petcock). Older scooters used manual petcocks to turn the fuel flow on and off. These older scooters usually have a "reserve" setting on the petcock. Sometimes if just a little gas remains in the tank, you have to turn the nozzle to "reserve." If you have a vintage scooter that is switched to reserve, make sure you fill up soon. If your scooter is properly tuned, you shouldn't have to twist the throttle to start it. Most older two-stroke engines, if you have a vintage scooter, have to be coaxed to start, so you may need to give it a bit of gas. Be careful not to flood the engine with gas! If you do, wait five to ten minutes before attempting to start your scooter again.

• **Key.** Turn the key on. Obvious, but essential.

• **Ignition cut-off switch.** If you have one of these on your bike, make sure it's not in the "off" position.

• **Battery.** First check to see if the leads to the battery are tight. Then, if you have a non-sealed battery, check through the transparent sides to see if your battery has enough liquid. If the level has gone down slightly, you can top it off with distilled water. If the liquid is very low, you have to get some battery acid, which is very dangerous stuff. Wear gloves, don't let it touch your body, and for heaven's sake don't breathe it in. If your battery is that low, though, check to see if the side is cracked or the top isn't tight. If the level hasn't fallen too low you may be able to

*Be careful not to flood the engine with gas! If you do, wait five to ten minutes before attempting to start your scooter again.*

Pop off the left side panel of a Vespa and find your spare tire and 12 volt battery. Don't forget to bring along wrenches in case you need to change a wheel on the side of the road.

recharge it. You may need to leave the battery attached to a trickle charger overnight.

• **Magneto.** If your scooter is vintage it may not have a battery, but a magneto. With a magneto there is less to worry about, but they do tend to age. There is a remote possibility that your magneto has lost its charge and has to be remagnetized. This is unlikely, however, so check everything else first.

• **Spark plugs.** Make sure your plug wire is tightly attached to the top of the spark plug. Consider checking the gap or changing the plug as described in the spark plug section of your owner's manual.

• **Choke.** If your scooter is equipped with a choke or fast-idle lever, you may have to choke the motor when the motor is cold. If the engine is still warm, however, you might not need to choke it. Turn off the choke as soon as the engine runs properly.

## NEW PLUGS?
## KEEPING THE SPARK ALIVE

After you've tried out all of the above tricks

and your scoot still won't start, roll up your sleeves and get out the wrenches.

The first potential problem to check off your list is compression. When you step on the kickstarter does it offer some resistance? If the kickstarter won't move, something could be blocking the piston and this requires major surgery. If the kickstarter gives far too easily, the piston rings could be shot and once again, you'll need to disassemble the cylinder. Fortunately, both of these problems are unlikely, especially with a modern scooter.

Next, pop off the side panel covering the carburetor. Close the petcock which controls the fuel line. Take a screwdriver and undo the line from the gas tank into the carburetor at the entrance to the carburetor. Once the screws are loose, pull off the tube. Turn on the petcock and gas should flow easily. If it doesn't, you have a fuel blockage even before gas reaches your carb.

Try reassembling the gas line and choking the scooter to allow more fuel. If you still aren't getting enough gas, you may have a blockage inside the carburetor and might have to rebuild it. Unfortunately, many vintage scooters didn't have any sort of fuel filter to prevent sediment in the tank from clogging up the carb. Modern scooters solved this simple problem.

Finally, check your sparkplug. Take off the side panel (usually the right one) and make sure that the plug wire is attached snugly to the top of the plug. If so, that's not your problem. Pop it off and remove the spark plug with your handy plug wrench. Check the gap with a spark plug gapper. The correct measurements are in your owner's manual. If your engine is hot, be very careful not to burn yourself. Examine the end of the spark plug and see which criteria it fits:

• **Black and oily.** If it's covered in thick oil, you have too much oil mixed in with your gas or could possibly have defective crankshaft seals. In a pinch, you can clean up the plug with a cloth and wire brush, but the plug should be replaced soon.

• **Wet but clean.** If the plug is moist without the gooey black oil, the engine is flooded and needs to air out. Wipe off the plug and screw it back into the cylinder. Secure the plug wire, replace the cowling, and give it another kick (but ease off on the throttle).

• **Rich and sooty.** If the plug is black but dry with a fine, powdery soot on it, there's too much gas in the air-gas mix of the carburetor. You need to adjust the jets of the carburetor. Either consult your owner's manual or stop in a shop.

• **Lean and white.** If the plug is white (and almost looks brittle), the air-gas mixture of your carburetor is giving the engine too much air and running the engine hot.

• **Tanned to perfection.** If the end of the plug is a light tan color, there's no problem with your plug or the tuning of your carburetor.

To make sure the plug is firing, pop the plug wire on the plug (without screwing it back into the cylinder). Ground the plug by placing its end against the metal of the motor and step on the kick starter. You should see a nice blue spark

When Piaggio decided to revive the PX series of its classic Vespa line, the company didn't stay entirely true to the old version—fortunately. Piaggio incorporated modern touches to a classic: 200 mm front disc brakes, a halogen headlamp, and a contoured saddle.

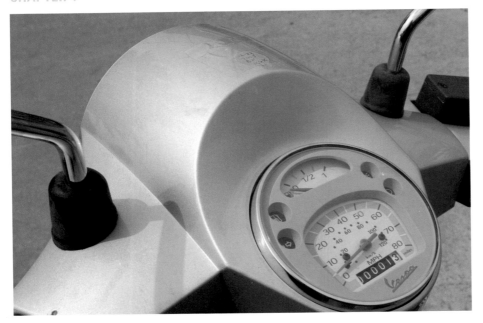

at the end of the plug, which indicates that the plug is fine.

If the spark is small and inconsistent, a larger ignition problem could be to blame. Repeat this procedure with a different plug to make sure it's not just the spark plug.

If you replace your spark plug, be sure to get the proper plug according to your owner's manual. Remember that the end of the plug is where the gasoline explodes, so you can't fudge it with incorrect gap or plug.

## CHANGING OIL: ENGINES NEED LUBRICANT

Two-stroke engines burn oil. Early scooters call for the rider to mix the oil right into the gas tank. Ideally, you should mix the gas and

The headsets on the revived PX series Vespas from Piaggio bear an uncanny resemblance to the 1980s models—albeit with the slick new Vespa logo.

The updated front wheels of the new Vespa PX 150 bear little resemblance to the original 1946 Vespa wheels purportedly from discarded World War II fighter planes built by Piaggio. The new hydraulic dampers stop that classic sinking Vespa feeling when braking too hard, too fast.

oil in a gas can before filling the tank, but who has time for that? Be very careful to mix the exact amount of oil to gas as called for in your owner's manual. If you don't, the engine will either run too hot (and could seize) or the spark plugs can foul from the extra oil. Once you fill up the tank, jiggle the scooter to and fro to slosh around the gas and oil inside.

Modern two-strokes have avoided the hassle of pre-mixing your oil with a separate oil tank. Nevertheless, you should check the oil gauge each time you fill up, if not more often. Some scooters, like Vespas, have a handy little oil sight glass below the seat that shows exactly how much oil is inside.

Some two-strokes, and most four-stroke scooters, will have a little dipstick to check the oil level. Simply pull off the dipstick, wipe it off, put it back in the hole, and pull it out again to get an exact reading. Only add enough oil to fill the tank to the appropriate level, which usually won't be very much oil.

Besides just keeping the oil level up, once at least every 5,000 miles you have to change the gearbox oil. Depending on the kind of scooter you own, the engine will require a different type of oil. Check your owner's manual for the proper weight oil for your scooter. To change the oil, a few steps are involved:

• **Drain.** On the bottom side of the engine, find the drain plug, which is usually a large bolt, sometimes an Allen-head. Put a large pan under the scooter to collect all the dirty oil. Use the correctly sized wrench (remember that European makes use metric), and loosen the bolt. Move your hands out of the way as the stream of oil fills the pan. Remember to remove the filler cap to ensure that all the oil drains. It also helps to drain the oil when the engine and transmission are warm, since warm oil flows more freely than cold oil. Just remember that when the oil is warm so is the engine, and when the engine is warm, the exhaust pipe is hot enough to cause severe burns. Be

**The new PX series of Vespa mixes the modern and the earliest scooters. One key to spotting the difference of the older and modern PX series is the newer seat and the "Vespa" insignia on the legshield that uses the older lettering (if a bit smaller).**

The 400cc engine of the Yamaha Majesty puts it well within the "maxi-scooter" category. The liquid-cooled, four-stroke engine needs this massive muffler to keep it quiet.

careful not to contact hot components when draining oil from a warm engine.

• **Filter.** If your bike has an oil filter, remove the old one. The scooter will either have a canister filter that requires you to loosen the screws (don't lose them!) or an automobile-style filter that just screws off. The filter will sometimes have some oil inside of it, so be careful to dump it into the pan with the dirty oil. Before putting on a new filter, be careful to dab some clean oil on the rubber seal to make a tight fit on the engine.

• **Oil.** Before filling up the engine with clean oil, clean and reinstall the drain plug. Most scooter makes will have a small magnet on the drain plug to catch any metal shavings. Be sure to remove any bits of metal before tightening.

After all the bolts are tightened, find the opening of the oil tank and fill it to the "full" mark (check the owner's manual beforehand to see how much oil the scooter generally needs). Once you've filled the oil to the full mark on the dipstick (if there is one), start the

scooter and let it idle for a bit. Turn off the engine and wait a minute. Check the oil level with the dipstick to make sure the level is correct. The level will likely have gone down because some of the oil you have filled will have been pumped into the oil filter. Refill the reservoir to the "full" level.

Do not dispose of old oil down the drain (it's toxic waste), but take it to a service station where they're usually happy to take if off your hands.

## TAMING YOUR TIRES: FIRST CONTACT TO THE GROUND
• **Wear and tear.** Get in the habit of giving a quick inspection of your tires before hitting the road. Check for any swelling, cuts, cracks, or rocks and nails embedded in the tread. Riding in the hot sun can speed up the wear on a tire, so one hard day of riding can take its toll. Once you notice your tires wearing thin, they are probably in much worse shape than they show. Change your worn-out tires to avoid a blowout

while zipping down the road or a slideout on a treadless tire on a rainy day.

•**Air pressure.** Before you throw your leg over the saddle seat, give a glance to the tires to see if they're sagging. If the tire's air pressure is low, the tire will wear faster and is more prone to being punctured. Carry an air gauge in your glove box. Learn what the maximum air pressure is from the side of the tire or your owner's manual. It's normal for your tire to lose a little bit of air pressure, so just pump it back up. Changes in temperature or altitude can affect the amount of air pressure in your tires. If your tire has lost a lot of air, you may have a slow leak or small puncture. Consider changing it before setting out on a trip.

•**Patching.** If you do indeed have a hole in your inner tube (provided you have a scooter with an inner tube—many modern scooters use tubeless tires), you can patch it using a bicycle tire patch kit. Before spending the time to do this little project, consider how much scooting time you

could lose if you have to spend it in a hospital bed. New tubes aren't very expensive. Avoid the synthetic tubes because they tend to blow when punctured as opposed to rubber tubes which will usually seal around a nail for a slow leak.

•**Size.** Most smaller scooter wheels use 10-inch tires, but early Vespas used elfin 8-inchers with an occasional 9-inch wheel to befuddle its owners. The width is generally 3 or 3.5 inches and replacements have to match exactly. Larger scooters generally have larger tires of anywhere from 12 inches on up. Look on the side of your tire or consult your owner's manual for exact size before plopping down the cash for replacements.

•**Spares.** If you're going on a long ride, having a spare tire along could save you having to find a tow and being stuck in some small town for days. Most vintage scooters either allow you to stow a spare tire under one of the sidepanels or have a rack for a spare tire you can install on the back of

*"Maybe your second car shouldn't be a car. Don't laugh, it makes a lot more sense to hop on a Vespa than it does to climb in a 4,000-lb. automobile to go half a mile for a 4-oz. pack of cigarettes."*
—Vespa ad from 1964

**The telescopic front fork on the Yamaha Majesty makes for a smooth ride. Notice the 267mm disc brake on the relatively large 14-inch wheel. Oddly enough, the rear wheel is only 13 inches.**

Finally, you've succeeded in wrenching your Vespa engine from the monocoque body only to discover that the motor is connected to the carb and wheel. Garden hose is extra.

Delving inside the clutch and brake assembly of a Vespa engine reveals the brilliance of Corradino d'Ascanio's design of wedging everything into tight spaces. After running up miles on your scooter, the engine will surely look dirtier than this. Remember to keep your workspace clean as any sand, dust or grime can be hazardous to your putt-putt's powerplant when you decided to see what lies being those bolts.

the scooter. Make sure your spare is properly inflated and that your glove box has the right-sized wrenches to change a flat.

• **Choosing a tire.** Scooter tires tend to be expensive (up to $100 each) because they are made in small batches compared to car tires that are made by the millions. Make sure you match the size of your new tire to the old one, and start shopping. Nowadays, a wide selection of tires is available with everything from classic whitewalls to vintage treads to racing tires filling the shelves. If you're restoring a bike, the tires are one element that absolutely need to be new if you plan on actually driving it. If you're using sport tires, check to make sure you put the tire on facing the correct direction, because some are uni-directional.

• **Changing a tire.** Ideally, you should bring your scooter into the shop and have them mount a new tire. Unfortunately, you'll probably be on the road when you discover this immediate need. Be sure to carry the right-sized wrenches (and a spare tire) in case you need to change a tire by the side of the road.

The method for changing a tire will vary with each model of scooter, so keep your owner's manual safely in the glove box (in a plastic bag). The first step is usually to unbolt the rim from the brake drum, at least on vintage scooters with drum brakes (most modern scooters use disc brakes). On many scooters, be careful which bolts you unfasten because you might accidentally dismantle the brakes instead. On modern scooters you simply need to remove the axle bolt and slide the axle out. Some scooters might require you to unbolt a shock absorber or exhaust pipe to make room to remove the axle. Once you've loosened these bolts or removed the axle, the rim and tire should pop off. If you have a spare, simply replace it.

If you have a modern scooter with a tubeless tire, you will now need to bring your tire into a shop to have a new tire mounted. Otherwise, to disassemble the tire, let the air all the way out. Remove any other nuts and bolts that hold the two pieces of the rim together.

Although a dismantled engine may seem an unhappy affair, at least Piaggio's ingenuity is laid bare as the air scoop cooling shroud (with a bit of red spray paint) encircles the engine to keep the piston from seizing.

*"The Vespa is a reliable piece of machinery. Its engine has only three moving parts. There's not much that can break. (People have driven Vespas over 100,000 miles without major repairs). And it's so simple to work on, a complete tune-up costs six dollars."*
—Vespa ad from 1964

Stephen Heller of Scooterville lubes up a scooter to hit the road. Most gas stations will have paper cones to aid with this delicate maneuver and avoid covering your scooter in viscous slime.

The only thing left holding the two pieces of the rim together at this point is rust and the rubber tire bead which has probably molded itself to the metal. A flat-head screwdriver will work to wedge the two pieces apart, but I recommend a hammer's claw or crowbar. Once the tire is apart, you can assess the damage to the inner tube and decide whether you need to replace the tube, tire, or both.

When reassembling the wheel, push the valve stem of the inner tube through its hole. Be careful not to pinch the inner tube between the wheel rims when reassembling. Sometimes filling up the inner tube slightly will prevent this problem. A light sprinkle of corn starch or baby powder on the inner tube will keep it from catching on

the rubber of the tire. Make sure that the two pieces of the rim correspond to where the valve stem goes. You may have to use pliers to hold the valve in place when inflating it slightly.

Put on the nuts, washers, and bolts; tighten in a criss-cross pattern; and inflate the tire to the maximum pressure indicated on the sidewall. Replace the wheel on the scooter and go!

## NEED MORE OOMPH? MODIFY FOR SPEED

If you modify one part of your scooter, you may have to update another part, and so on. Talk to friends who have tricked out their scooter. Consult your local scooter shop for advice and possible future changes you'll have to make to your ride. With those caveats in mind, here's an abridged list of possible modifications:

• **Engine.** People building hot-rod cars have an old saying: "There's no substitute for cubic inches." When discussing scooters, it might be better to rephrase that old saw with: "There's no substitute for cubic centimeters." However you state it, the saying holds true, and the surest way to obtain more power is to have a piston that displaces more air. Because of that, there are many kits available to increase the capacity of most popular small scooter engines.

Many kits allow you to punch out your 49-cc engine to 70-cc or 80-cc, but beware—not all kits are created equal. Research any potential kit on the Internet or at local scooter shops before plunking down the money to punch out your 50-cc Zuma to a 125-cc monster. One of the crit-ical factors with two-stroke engine kits is oiling. A 49-cc engine has different oiling requirements than an 80-cc engine. If you plop a big-bore cylinder on your small-bore engine without modifying your oil system to match the new cylinder, your scooter will be extremely fast for about an afternoon. After that you will be rebuilding a seized engine.

Before pulling out your engine in hopes of customizing it for more power, ask yourself how much power you want or need, if you're willing to adjust the body-work of your bike, and how much time and money you want to spend. Some scooterists will wedge a 250-cc engine into a little 50 cc scooter for super power on a puny bike. These experiments are usually best left in the hands of mechanical geniuses rather than homespun garage hobbyists.

You can probably make most kits work on most engines, but it's best to find an

Pay heed to fill up the tank with the proper liquid: oil or gas. Modern scooters mix the oil themselves and don't involve any of that pesky pre-mix *miscela* made famous at Italian gas stations. Don't use any ol' motor oil, but check your owner's manual or scooter for the best brand for your scoot and don't use four-stroke oil in a two-stroke engine!

To offset the "Aix-to-Ghent lean" of an engine that rests on the right side, Piaggio placed the spare tire and battery on the left. Unfortunately, this tilting problem has plagued Piaggio's Vespas but makes scooter-spotting easy for newbies.

While Lambrettisti with their magnetos may gloat about never having to worry their pretty heads over a dead battery, at least the lights on modern scooters stay bright and horns scare deviant felines in their path. The downside of batteries, however, is keeping them at full capacity. A trickle charger left overnight can revitalize an otherwise inert 12 volt (assuming the liquid inside is topped off).

Pop open the sidepanel and hope that your Vespa motor will look so tidy. Notice the dull-colored cooling shroud which also protects the engine from mucking up with grime.

An easy fix for the novice mechanic is popping off the air cooler and cleaning out the dust or replacing it. Beware of over-tightening the bolts and crunching the fresh filter.

engine modification kit specifically for your scooter. Some of the requirements usually involve having to bore out the cylinder, get a new piston and rings, modify the ports to accommodate the adjustments, set the ignition timing, rejet the carburetor, modify the gearing on the oil pump to provide adequate oiling for the new displacement, and get a new spark plug. This is best left to a qualified scooter mechanic. Sometimes you can pull off the engine and ship the whole shebang to a scooter shop for the modifications.

• **Exhaust pipes.** One of the simplest ways to get extra power out of your scooter is to install a performance muffler (called an "expansion chamber" in two-stroke engines), but if you mount an exhuast that is too loud you'll have to deal with angry neighbors, miffed cops, and hearing loss. Your stock exhaust that was designed specifically for your scooter is probably the best all around system. Some aftermarket mufflers, however, will increase your power at low speed (but may give you less at high rpms). Be wary of slick-looking chrome pipes because that smooth finish may crack after being exposed to constant heat. Sometimes the best exhaust to put on your scooter is just a new stock exhaust because the old one may be clogged with soot, dirt, or fuel that worked its way through the engine.

• **Carburetor.** Putting a larger carburetor on your scooter is another way of getting a bit more power. Often the next engine size up in your line (i.e. 125-cc vs. 150-cc) will have the carburetor you need. Also, check into carbs from small-engine motorcycles, as they may use the carbs you need and be much cheaper than those off a scooter. Usually, you should only put on the next-size-up carburetor, and you'll need to put in new jets. Because your engine is smaller than the engine for which the carburetor was initially made, you'll probably have to experiment with the settings for the

Stephen "Hell-Cat" Heller tops off the tank of a black Vespa for a customer at Scooterville in Dinkytown, Minnesota. High on the list of items to check if your damn scooter won't start is the obvious fuel problem. Sometimes a bit of gas remains in the bottom of the tank, but is below the regular fuel level. Simply flip the petcock to "reserve," and zoom to the 7-11 for a fill-up. Better yet, keep a gas tank in your garage.

new jets because they might not correspond to the manual. You might even have to scrap your old manifold and air cleaner for one that will fit the carb.

Before you invest in a new carburetor, be sure that all of these new components will still fit under the side panel.

• **Brakes.** After you've modified your bike, or at least tuned it to run at its best, you may notice that you need more braking power. Usually the best answer is making sure your existing brakes are working correctly, replacing the brake pads, and lubricating the brake cables. At your scooter shop, ask about newer brake pads that are often grooved to reduce the amount of dust inhibiting the stopping power. Older scooters used drum brakes before the disc brake was finally introduced with the Lambretta TV in the 1960s. These early disc brakes weren't nearly as effective as present-day discs, which come standard on most modern scooters. Kits to put disc brakes on your classic scooter are

available, but beware that they may not fit easily under the bodywork and that you may have to hide a hydraulic system somewhere on the fork.

## EXCEEDING 30 MILES PER HOUR: TRICKING OUT 50-CC SCOOTERS

While 50-cc scooters may seem small and slow, they have actually been tuned down to be that way. With modern technology, these engines are actually very efficient and fast. After all, Italy has 50-cc cars for teenagers and elderly people who have lost their regular driving license. A modern 50-cc engine is a far cry from the 50-cc engine of 50 years ago. Because many countries don't require license plates, registration, or a license to drive a 50-cc scooter or moped, the engines have actually been dumbed down so as not to exceed a certain speed limit (usually 30 miles per hour).

With a little handiwork, you or your scooter shop can de-restrict the engine to allow it to work to its full capacity. The

Modern scooters—like modern automobiles—have myriad plastic shrouds to protect the engine and moveable parts from road sludge. Before accessing the engine, pull out the ratchet and see what lies beneath.

Time for a final drive oil change. Pop off the side panel, unscrew the plastic shroud (if applicable) and start searching for the drain plug at the bottom of the engine block.

people who know the most about your scooter are usually at the dealership. They will know exactly how to modify your bike so it can live up to its potential. The dealer will probably not be *allowed* to do this, so this is where you charm the mechanics or have them do it "on the side" for you—as long as you don't tell. Often, the mechanics will instead tell you exactly what to do (take notes!) for your model, because they would lose their jobs if they did it themselves. To get them to talk, tease them that they're acting like it's their moral duty to stand up for restricting scooters to 30 miles per hour. If they still refuse to divulge the secrets, ask your local independent scooter shop for help. They'll be happy to do it for you. If these approaches don't work, do a little Internet research.

Two or three pieces stand in the way of you passing cars on your 50-cc scooter. Apart from replacing the exhaust, here are two ways to trick out your scooter.

• **Replace** one of the small carburetor jets with a larger one.

• **Remove** a simple washer in the variator that prevents the scooter going into its highest gearing.

Before you pull out the wrenches to de-restrict your scooter, however, some warnings are due:

• **Outlaw scooter.** If you take off the restrictions, you may be in violation of your state's or country's laws; however, there's very little chance you'd ever get caught (unless they clock you going 50 miles per hour or deconstruct your scooter). You may have to register your newly modified 50-cc scooter as a motorcycle because it can now exceed 30 miles per hour. You will likely need a motorcycle endorsement on your license and your insurance could go up, as well, but since you took my advice and passed the MSF RiderCourse, you probably have this already, so no problems there.

• **Void the warranty.** Taking off the restriction on your little scooter could effectively cancel the warranty on it. You need to decide if it's worth it to get to church on time.

## REPLACING THE CLUTCH: WHEN SHIFTING WEARS THIN

The word "clutch" refers to different parts on different types of scooters. On scooters with manual transmissions, the clutch is a sequence of spring-loaded plates that are pressed together to engage the gears with the crankshaft. On such scooters the clutch is an essential part of making the scooter run smoothly. Many modern scooters have forgone the clutch in favor of automatic (or twist-n-go) systems that spare the scooterist from tiresome shifting. On this type of scooter, the clutches are centrifu- gally-operated pullies that act on the drive belt to vary the transmission ratio of power to the rear wheel. This is much like the system used on snowmobiles and modern autos equipped with continuously variable transmissions (CVTs).

On manually-shifted scooters, the clutch allows much more control of the engine and how much power is used. For example, keeping the scooter in a lower gear with high rpms gives more power and can help you up a steep hill. While automatic scooters are just downright easier to drive, geared scooters are generally faster and have more control.

You can modify a modern automatic scooter to give you more control with a clutch kit. Such kits use different parts to alter the changing of the gear ratio. It sounds complicated, and since the mathamatical formula involves the use of pi, it is also complicated from a geometric point of view, but in practice, it is simple. With a clutch kit you gain more acceleration off the line, usually at the sacrifice of top speed.

One of the drawbacks of geared scooters is that the clutch can wear out. If you pull back on the clutch lever and it comes back too easily and makes it hard to shift, you've got troubles. Most likely, you'll just need to tighten the clutch cable so it engages more easily.

If the scooter is old, though, you may need to replace the clutch. Listen for

**Locating the drain plug is never an easy task for the novice. Look for the lowest nut on the engine and give it a turn (in this case it's the horizontal brass bolt). The bolt will usually be magnetized to attract any metal shavings from the engine. Clean these off before reinserting the bolt.**

Once you've found the drain plug, wrench off the nut. Be prepared, however, as the oil may flow over hand and wrench onto yon floor. Keep a drain pain at the ready—in this case, a handy I-Can't-Believe-It's-Not-Butter bowl—and bring the soiled oil to the local mechanic's shop for recycling. This is toxic waste, so dumping it down the drain can cause the Feds to come knocking or at least leave you with a guilty conscience for killing all those ducks.

unusual rattling noises when you disengage the clutch. If you notice that shifting has suddenly become more difficult (and tightening the cable does nothing), replace the clutch before you get stranded or are forced to grind the gears to get home. On most scooters, special tools are required to pop off the clutch. Consult your owner's manual and be careful not to lose the springs.

## SCOOTER CUSTOMIZING: MODDING OUT YOUR BIKE

British Mods will forever be associated with oodles of mirrors and lights jutting from the legshield like rays from the sun. Actually, Mod scooter style varied from year to year, with some riders espousing perfect stock scooters to others hot rodding the engine and stripping off all the bodywork for an almost Rocker-like motorcycle look. In general, though, Mods were keen on any accessory that could be tacked on the ride. Since that is the style immortalized in the

film *Quadrophenia*, that is the style most people associate with the Mods. Here's some of the favorite Mod modifications:

• **Two-tone color scheme.** Often the side panels, horn cover, front fender, and handlebars were painted a darker hue, perhaps in reverence of American two-tone cars of the 1950s.

• **Lights and horns.** Fed up with dimming tail and headlamps and inaudible horns that functioned well only at high rpms due to magnetos, Mods often rigged up an extra 6- or 12-volt battery in the glove box or under the seat to provide juice for dozens of lights and long chrome horns.

• **Mirrors.** Affixing the mirrors to the legshield and handlebars required near genius mechanical prowess. Often the mirrors extended more than a foot past the edge of the sidepanel. The untold secret is that most scooters shake so much when riding that the long-stemmed mirrors are more decorations than anything else.

• **Wheel rack and covers, rear back rest, and front rack.** Any accessory is worth the price as long as it's covered in chrome.

• **Chrome.** Only so many lights and mirrors could be fastened on to the legshield, so some Mods opted to chrome as much of the scooter as they could afford. Others dreamed of gold-plating their scooter just like the gold Lambretta given to Jayne Mansfield for appearing in Innocenti ads.

• **Foxtails, leopard skin seat covers, and fur trim.** A scooter that isn't somehow customized with good luck charms, banners, or other mascots is only a blank canvas awaiting personality.

Getting the right amount of engine oil into the motor can be risky guesswork without the proper tools. Some scooters allow the mechanic to simply top off the oil in the engine to a certain level, at which point it can't take any more liquid. More likely, however, is that you need to measure the exact amount and then insert. In this photo, Stephen Heller uses a handy syringe, but ma's turkey baster can suffice in a pinch.

**Chapter 5**

# SCOOTER STYLE

## WHAT YOU WILL LEARN

- How to dress like a modern San Fran Mod
- Vespa bath salts and perfume really do exist
- How Italian women refused to sit sidesaddle and insisted on driving their own scooters
- The mindset of the Mod—from Northern Soul to pill popping
- That "Rockers look just like Elvis, only worse"

*Accessorize for Speed*
As in the fashion world, accessorizing your look is the key to dressing for success. With scooters and their puny top speeds, you can't always drive fast, so you must at least look like you're driving at maximum velocity. This 1950's Vespa is decked out for piazza cruising with so many aftermarket accessories that it attracts *carabinieri* to write up a speeding ticket even while it's parked: Chrome trinkets, shiny but nonfunctional engine trim, big-lipped bumper overriders, wire headlamp stoneguards, whitewall Pirelli tires, spare wheel with leatherette cover, metallic cable covers, and a St. Christopher's medal are almost essential as a starting point. In the land of bolt-on chrome exhaust extenders, you can never accessorize too much.
*Collezione Vittorio Tessera*

Everyone from Skinheads to Mods to liberated women have declared the scooter their steed. Rallies went from pleasant social gatherings in the 1950s to anti-social riots during the May Day bank holidays of 1964.

### "A NEW RACE OF GIRLS"
Scooters were designed with women in mind. *Popular Mechanics* wrote in 1947, "As the family's second 'car,' the scooter makes shopping a pleasure for the housewife."

Apart from being just a tool to further the wife's bond to her suburban stove, scooters emancipated women ever since Amelia Earhart was pictured on top of a Motoped. Female suffragists would zip down U. S. sidewalks on these dangerous little Autopeds, just as their British counterparts stepped on the running board of ABC Skootamotas in the 1910s.

When the scooter flew south postwar, Italians added the spice. Unabashed Italian

divas like Gina Lollobrigida and Anna Magnani hopped on a Vespa and blew smoke in the face of passersby, or as a 1954 *Picture Post* article wrote about "'A New Race of Girls,' untamed, unmanicured, proud, passionate, bitter Italian beauties [on their] clean, sporting Vespa.... "

In fact, when Piaggio designer Corradino D'Ascanio assembled the first Vespa, the gas tank was removed from its position between the rider's legs so dresses could be easily worn. Citing this improved design, the *New York Times Magazine* wrote in 1958 that, "Another visible difference is that scooters do not have a center bar for the driver to straddle." The article continued by referencing Robert Browning's equestrian poem of jockeys riding from Belgium to the south of France. "This makes for more girl riders and less Ghent-to-Aix forward lean." Since many gussied-up Italian women insisted on high heels, the motor-

cycle foot shifter was left by the wayside, replaced by a hand shifter to simplify dropping your wasp into a higher gear.

As scooter designs meshed with women's clothes, fashion changed as well to maximize riding ease. "The narrowing of the new-look skirt was dictated in order to prevent it getting tangled up with the wheels. The slipper shoe was created for footplate comfort. The turtleneck sweater and neckerchief were designed against draughts on the neck," according to *Picture Post* of 1950. Trousers were soon the rage, since skirts would inevitably blow back, and handkerchiefs kept new moptop hairdos in place. Sunglasses became a cool necessity, as well as keeping bugs out of the rider's eyes—even more dangerous than not

looking hip.

Scooter fashion hit the Milanese runways with designer Emilio Pucci leading the way in 1949, and the fickle fashion biz rediscovered this "new look" every few years with Anna Sui and others finally putting models back on scooters in 1995. Innocenti's prudish newsletter *Lambretta Notizario* couldn't stand these fashion faux pas and lamented that "one is all too frequently tormented by the sight of badly trousered women on motor scooters."

In spite of the obvious design of scooters for women, magazine articles inevitably placed her on the pillion seat—usually in a dangerous side-saddle position—as in a 1957 *Popular Mechanics* article, "Two persons can ride one at the

*"In the early 1960s…scooters were displayed (and sometimes sold) not in car or motor-cycle showrooms but in exclusive 'ladies' fashion shops. They were thought to be a good thing to dress a window with, regarded less as a means of transport than as chic metal accessories, as jewelry on wheels."*

—Dick Hebdige in "Object as Image: The Italian Scooter Cycle"

## BEAUTY CONTEST:
## MISS VESPA DARLING vs. MISS LAMBRETTA

In the 1960s, both Piaggio and Innocenti (separately, of course) sponsored international beauty contests on scooters, noting that a well-tended putt-putt added much to a tidy image. In Britain, famous movie stars presented the Silver Rose Bowl award to the Miss Vespa Darling. At the English Lambretta National Rally held in Portsmouth, the winner of the Miss Lambretta contest would go on to compete in the prestigious Miss Lambretta International contest.

By this time, Piaggio and Innocenti both financed massive advertising campaigns to promote "scooter culture" in general, and their respective vehicles in particular. The Vespa was advertised as the second conquering of the New World by a Genovese (the first being by Italian Christopher Columbus, not Leif Erikson). Owners' magazines funded by the companies were published in different languages, containing articles on the latest updates, movie stars on scooters, and conti-

nental tours. These publications pushed the idea that the sleek, attractive scooter was fashionable but functional: fashionable, because no bar between the rider's legs meant the rider could wear the latest styles instead of riding gear, and the covered engine prevented oil from spotting their clothes; functional because a scooter could tour the world but still be parked anywhere.

Piaggio and Innocenti were no longer advertising a product. They were promoting a lifestyle.

same time, but a woman wearing a skirt (particularly if it is a straight one) must ride sidesaddle if she is the passenger." In that same year, a Vespa accessory catalog even featured a painfully uncomfortable *Poltrovespa* sidesaddle seat with a backrest.

A 1957 article in *National Geographic* on Italy featured a woman on a scooter, but relegated her to the back seat in the text. "Women ride, too. When papa drives, mamma sits sidesaddle on the box seat, often with a baby in her lap. Youngsters stand between seat and handlebars."

According to Dick Hebdige, male British Mods had the same attitude and often belittled their girlfriends as mere "pillion fodder." In the United States, attitudes in the monthly *American Mercury* in 1957 weren't much better, ". . . young couples, she riding sidesaddle prettily and revealingly and he, heading deliberately for every bump to jounce her into holding him tighter.... "

While the media put women on the pillion, scooter companies were more than happy to have them in the driver's seat,

*Rumble in Brighton*
Brutish British rockers on their grimy, uncouth working-class Triumphs taunt a line of Mods on their Italian hairdryers during the 1964 Brighton Beach Bank Holiday fracas that shocked Great Britain in this still from the film *Quadrophenia*. The movie summed up the Mod lifestyle to the sounds of The Who with Pete Townshend's Rickenbacker and HiWatt cranked to 11 and harmonizing with packs of Vespas and Lambrettas at full, unmuffled, two-stroke bore. Italian suits, army parkas, and scooters were the signs of the times.

*Rocker Scooter*

BSA-Triumph teamed up to build identical scooters—the Triumph Tigress and BSA Sunbeam—each in two versions: a 175cc two-stroke single and a 250cc four-stroke twin. The 250cc engines pushed the scooters faster than the 10-inch wheels and 5-inch drum brakes were made to handle. The Mod market deemed these British-made scooters (by motorcycle manufacturers no less!) unworthy, and sales plummeted. The Tigress and Sunbeam attempted to thwart the Italian-dominated scooter market but by 1960 much of the craze had faded away. The Tigress and Sunbeam unfortunately died a quick death.

since it meant a whole new market. Innocenti ads featured women everywhere on scooters, and while the annual Piaggio calendars consisted of cheesecake snapshots, at least the women were *driving* the Vespas, as opposed to motorcycle calendars with women in skimpy bikinis sprawled across the bikes awaiting their leathered Rocker.

Innocenti actually turned the tables on the backseat rider in a 1954 advertising film *Travel Far, Travel Wide*, echoing Amelia Earhart's famous photo on a Motoped. A shiny new Vespa is on the runway as a stewardess gets off the plane and on to her putt-

putt, "The air hostess can become the pilot herself—and there's plenty of room on that pillion for a friend!" The male pilot then hops on the pillion and women's emancipation is complete.

## IN MOD WE TRUST

In London's lower-class East End, the Mod rebellion took root. Teenagers with a little extra loot in their pockets from part-time jobs hit the classy shops on Carnaby Street for the latest Italian styles to one-up their mates. Mods took formal fashion to the extreme by being far better dressed than

The battle to stay in vogue was intense as Mods studied the latest magazines and tuned in religiously to *Ready, Steady, Go!*, a TV show featuring the "with-it" bands of the week from The Small Faces to the Hollies and an opening shot of a scooter. While being bored stiff during the week, Mods would count the hours to the weekend. When the whistle blew and work let out, the two-stroke exhaust filled the air and the dancehalls rocked with Northern Soul. "At the moment we're hero-worshipping the Spades—they can dance and sing. . ." said a Mod in 1964 in the book *Generation X* by Hamblett and Deverson.

Sleep was irrelevant as pill-poppers downed their "blues" and shook to the "Lambretta Twist" all night long. While Rockers wallowed in ale, "[Mods] were a little *too* smart, somewhat *too* alert, thanks to amphetamines," according to Hebdige.

In typical "reefer madness" hype, the *Sunday Mirror* in 1964 ran a feature "Exposing the Drug Menace" with a large photo of a Drinamyl pill bottle. Frightening parents that their kids would be dead within a few years unless they stopped their drug use, "They began by experimenting with purple hearts and other pep-pills, then progress via 'reefers' (marijuana) to heroin and cocaine—the two drugs that almost always lead to death before the age of thirty-five."

In Dick Hebdige's *Subculture*, he wrote that "pills medically prescribed for the treatment of neuroses were used as ends-in-themselves, and the motor scooter, originally an ultra-respectable means of transport, was turned into a menacing symbol of group solidarity."

## VESPA-LAMBRETTA WARS

The essential Mod fashion accessory was the scooter, preferably a Lambretta or Vespa. Piaggio's scooters were the first to cross the English Channel. Claude McCormack, the head of the Douglas firm, began importing Vespas into Britannia adding a chrome "Douglas" above the Vespa logo on the legshield. By 1951, Piaggio had licensed Douglas to build British Vespas and the 125-cc 2L2 Douglas

*Quadrophenia*!
**To witness the classic scooters in your city, just wait for the local revivalist movie theater (in this case, Minneapolis' Oak Street Cinema) to screen The Who's *Quadrophenia*. Slip on your best shark skin suit or tight tweed dress and head for the front row to laugh at Sting as a boot-licking bell boy while Pete Townshend smashes another Rickenbacker.**

even uptight upper-class fops. Materialism was the Mod cry, as each object purchased was turned into a fashion statement and object of rebellion. Rather than rejecting consumption like so many other youth movements before, the Mods were a "grotesque parody of the aspirations of [their] parents. . . who used goods as 'weapons of exclusion,'" according to historian Dick Hebdige. To have cool stuff was to flaunt it.

Vespa hit the streets of London by March. While Mods wouldn't latch on to the smooth Italian styling of Vespas for a few years, the stage was nevertheless set for the Lambretta-Vespa wars.

Innocenti's scooters invaded England when the Agg family set up a huge distribution network with a massive marketing campaign and many more dealers and repair shops than Douglas Vespa. Rather than constructing a factory to actually stamp out scooters in the U.K., the Agg family cashed in on the "Made in Italy" status. Anything Italian was in vogue, or as historian Dick Hebdige said of the Mods, "He is English by birth, Italian by choice."

While Douglas Vespas usually were quite a bit cheaper than the latest Lambretta, the models weren't updated annually, since remachining the British factory every year would stymie profits. Piaggio showrooms would only stock a few of the imported, speedy GS scooters, since they were more expensive to ship; rather, they preferred selling a home-bred Douglas Vespa.

Lambrettas earned a reputation as the faster of the two scooters, since window displays would feature only the quickest, latest models—especially the Lambretta TV 175 Series 2 (not the Series 1 lemon). To show their team loyalty, "The Blue Boys" wore their blue Lambretta Club colors to demonstrate that they absolutely wouldn't ride Vespas.

Unwilling to go softly into that good night, or even be put at second place, the larger Piaggio company released its gorgeous GS 160 Vespa in 1962, the pinnacle of Vespadom. In 1963, Innocenti responded to the British market and the Isle of Man scooter races with the TV 200 (aka GT 200), which provoked Piaggio's SS120, then Innocenti's SX200, and so on.

While Piaggio and Innocenti were battling for horsepower, most Mods were busy attaching any accessory they could screw onto their scooters. A British ad for scooter accessories wrote in huge letters, "Go Gay!" and featured a Lambretta decked out with flags, plaid seat covers, a windscreen, plaid saddlebags, and every piece of chrome that could fit.

"[A]ll these extras would slow the bike down considerably, although this didn't bother Mods as speed wasn't their priority, the slower you go, the more people see you," according to the Mod handbook *Empire Made*. Certain accessories were deemed "cool" and others certainly uncool—most likely from last year's model. Oversized windscreens and flags were definitely passé, while chrome crashbars, lights, and mirrors were hip—at least for the moment.

Two-tone styling came to scooters via Eddy Grimstead's shop on Barking Road in London. Soon Innocenti offered standard two-tone paint schemes to the British market, and each dealer offered their own styling with names like "Imperial," "Hurricane," "Z-Type," and "Mona."

**Accessorize for Speed**
Covering the classic Vespa with every bit of chrome, horn, or banner, this American scooter aficionado is ready for a rally in Rudesheim, Germany.

*"The pocket handkerchief fashion which swept the women's world in 1949 was devised to keep a pillion girl's hair tidy at speed... Next year, the blown hair problem was solved by the urchin cut."*
—*"A New Race of Girls"* Picture Post
*September 5, 1954*

**Scooting in Heels**
Try riding a Triumph motorcycle with a dress and heels and you'll understand why scooters appealed to women. Covering the motor with side panels and placing a full legshield on the front fork keeps the *signorina* clean for a night out on the town. With the extra accessories of chrome fender and sidepanel bars, the scooter paint scheme is protected from tipping as well.

While the average Mod could hardly afford to spring for a new scoot every year, a few simple tricks ensured a state-of-the-art scooter, at least in looks. While older Vespa side panels were hinged on to the scooter, Lambretta panels could easily be replaced with the current year's model. Since almost all scooter keys were identical, a black market scooter trade soon flourished in London. Even the notoriously unreliable Lambretta TV Series 1 were purchased and then made to look like new with the latest side panels, a bench seat, and chrome accessories. Soon only a trained eye could determine a scooter's make since "For every genuine GT200 there

were several alleged GT200s of dubious origins," according to *Empire Made*.

## ROCKERS' REBELLION

"Hey Johnny, what are you rebelling against?"

"Whatta ya got?" Marlon Brando in *Wild One*.

While Mods were busy exchanging styling cues and twisting to Northern Soul, their arch-enemies, the Rockers, were dropping a shilling in the Ace Bar jukebox, kick-starting their Café Racers, and making the rounds before the song ended. The lines were drawn and teenagers had to choose which side they were on. "You've got to be either a Mod or a Rocker to mean anything," said a Mod quoted in one of the British tabloids in 1964.

The dawn of the Rockers can be traced back to "American motorcycling's Day of Infamy" in Hollister, California in 1947 (according to Harry Sucher's *Harley-Davidson*) when a Time/Life photographer staged a photo of a member of the Booze Fighters on a Harley acting drunk with emptied beer bottles strewn on the floor.

Harley-Davidson was embarrassed, and the public was outraged. How could

---

## MOD DRESS: MACKINTOSH AND ANORAKS

While Rockers were busy wearing cowboy hats, leather jackets, flying boots, and bandanas, Mods were obsessed with slick Italian suits. Tailored to be tight-fitting with pegged legs and thin lapels, these shark skin suits were complemented by perfectly ironed shirts and a thin tie. Casual dress called for Fred Perry with the laurel wreath logo (or later, Munsingwear shirts with the little penguin). Sharing a styling cue with the Beats, "sometimes French berets were worn to stress the affiliation with the Continent and to further distinguish the 'scooter boys' from the Rockers," according to cultural theorist Dick Hebdige.

An early Mod in Colin MacInnes' book *Absolute Beginners* dressed more like a Dandy or Teddy Boy than the later Mods. The protagonist, Dean, is described as having "college-boy smooth crop hair with burned-in parting, neat white Italian rounded-collar shirt, short Roman jacket very tailored (two little vents, three buttons), no turn-up trousers with seventeen-inch bottoms absolute maximum, pointed toe shoes, and a white mac folded by his side."

MacInnes introduces his characters by their clothes, as telling of their personality. Dean's girlfriend rests unnamed, but her dress is described in detail. "Short

hem lines, seamless stockings, pointed toe high-heeled stiletto shoes, crepe nylon rattling petticoat, short blazer jacket, hair done up into the elfin style. Face pale-corpse colour with a dash of mauve, plenty of mascara."

In spite of these specific details on how to dress Mod, the clothes that eventually became most associated with the style (at least for men) were crepe-soled Hush Puppies or desert boots and olive green anoraks. Perhaps the hooded parka became engraved in the British public mind after Mods rode to Margate and Brighton in their rain gear and splashed their image across the tabloids in the battle with the Rockers. The 1979 film *Quadrophenia* further cemented the image of the pill-popping Mod in the oversized anorak to keep off the incessant English rain.

---

these motorcycles that provided such patriotic service during the war be transformed into a rebellious tool? Hollywood cashed in on the evil but enticing menace with *The Wild One* in 1953, with quotes from Cathy "the square."

"I've never ridden on a motorcycle before. It's fast. It scared me, but I forgot everything. It felt good." In trying to understand the boyish but beautiful rebel, Cathy prods Johnny (Marlon Brando):

Cathy: "What do you do? I mean, do you just ride around or do you go on some sort of picnic or something?"

Johnny: "A picnic? Man, you are too square. I have to straighten you out. Now listen, you don't go any one special place, that's cornball style. You just go! [snaps his fingers]. A bunch gets together after all week. It builds up. The idea is to have a ball. Now, if you gonna stay cool, you gotta wail. You gotta put something down. You gotta make some jive. Don't you know what I'm talking about?"

Just as the Mods studied magazines and movies to perfect their style, the British Rockers carefully copied the American movement adding typical English flair to what digressed into the Hell's Angels in America. In Johnny Stuart's great testament *Rockers*, he describes the style: "Then comes the scarf. . . It was stolen from American Cowboy movies. . . the Rocker begins to take on something of the Cowboy's identity as a wanderer, tramp, hobo; a bit of a villain too."

Elvis was an early Rocker hero, although driving a shiny 1956 red and white KH Harley rather than a souped up BSA or Norton Café Racer. This was too much for 17-year-old Mod Terry Gordon, as quoted in the *Daily Mirror* in 1964, "Rockers look like Elvis Presley, only worse." She went on to describe her horror of the Rocker aesthetic, "Mod girls don't wear any makeup—only foundation. Rocker girls use a lot of bright pink lipstick and piles of makeup."

Not only were Rockers scorned by Mods, but the media was wary, like *Mechanix Illustrated* in 1956, "Motorcycle people aren't used to dealing with the

general public. Some of them may give you a hard time if you don't look like one of the Wild Ones."

## THE BATTLE OF BRIGHTON

1964 was a banner year for delinquency. In California, the Attorney General released a notorious—and mostly fabricated—report on "Hoodlum Activities" and what to look for in a rebel: "…an embroidered patch of a winged skull wearing a motorcycle helmet…. Many affect beards and their hair is usually long and unkempt. Some wear a

*Scooter Rainbow*
**Like candy in a candy shop, this line of Vespas (and a lone Lambretta) haphazardly parked downtown St. Paul during a scooter rally circa 1996. No more dour black or olive green.**

**Square Vespa**
In the mid-1960s, Piaggio followed Lambretta's lead of the squared-off Slimline by introducing the speedy Vespa GT with a trapezoidal headlamp. This scooter makes its home along the Amalfi Coast, the perfect destination for turning around hairpin curves with hundred-foot drops to the sea below. No wonder composer Richard Wagner opted for a donkey to haul his puffy Germanic body up the hill rather than risking a ride on a sporty Vespa.

**Lambretta TV 175**
The ultimate mod machine was the souped-up Turismo Veloce 175 Series II with extra mirrors and lights attached to the mandatory roll bar. This second series of TV Lambrettas raised the headlamp to the handlebars to follow the turning wheel. The TV would again follow the Li's lead in 1962 with the slimline styling of the sixties.

single earring in a pierced ear lobe…. Some clubs provide that initiates shall be tattooed…. Another patch worn by some members bears the number '13'."

Across the Atlantic, Innocenti was planning a picnic. Any self-respecting Mod kick-started the Lammie and hit the beaches of Brighton for a bank holiday on May Day. "We will fight them on the beach," became the Churchill-mocking rallying cry as hyped-up Mods, thanks to amphetamnies, met their nemesis, the Rockers. Throwing deck chairs and punches amidst sunbathers, the Mods and the Rockers dueled as the bobbies tried to subdue them and the tabloids smiled, knowing they had a headline for tomorrow's edition.

Innocenti and Piaggio were horrified as their docile scooters became a tool of the

## PUTT-PUTT ODDITIES
## THE DUSTBIN: THE CAR ON TWO WHEELS

Scooterists atop Vespas and Lambrettas dismissed the most powerful scooter of the time, the Maico Mobile, as the "dustbin." The maker of Maico (short for Maisch and Co.) resided in "A peaceful section of the South German countryside, in which both the main works at Pfäffingen and the Maico Engine Works at Herrenberg are situated," according to 1955 Maico information bulletin. Postwar, Pfäffingen was in the French section of Germany and the factory was reduced to making toys for tots. Then in 1951, the phoenix rose from its ashes with the mammoth Maico Mobile that "will prove to be the true touring machine of the future," according to H. W. Boensch in 1951. "This prediction has now proved correct," claimed happy Maico ad men in 1955 for the most outlandish scooter to ever hit the Autobahn. For once, brochures about the "Car on Two Wheels" could be trusted when they wrote, "This was to be in no sense a copy of an existing machine, but rather a completely new vehicle suited to German weather conditions."

Although its successor had to live in the enormous shadow of the Dustbin, the Maicoletta was one of the fastest, most solid scooters ever built. Designers Pohl and Tetzlaff worked by candlelight in complete secrecy to unveil the 175-cc and 250-cc Maicoletta in 1955, which was soon equipped with a tremendous 275-cc engine putting 14 horsepower into the little chassis, making it the most powerful scooter in Germany. Now both the Maico scooters are prized possessions for collectors, and old-time Vespa and Lambretta enthusiasts are probably kicking themselves for not seeing the light when the Dustbin was in the showroom.

*"The lack of the helmet allowed long hair to blow freely back into the wind, and this, with the studded and ornamented jackets, and the aggressive style of riding, gave the motorbike boys a fearsome look which amplified the wildness, noise, surprise and intimidation of the motorbike.... The high cattlehorn handlebars, the chromium-plated mudguards gave the bikes an exaggerated look of fierce power."*
—Paul Willis writing about British Rockers in Birmingham

**Just about every type of widget imaginable is available to accessorize your scooter, from vintage chrome gewgaws to modern electrical conveniences.**

Cheesecake and scooters complement each other as seen by this naughty nurse at a vintage scooter rally near Minnehaha Falls.

*"The narrowing of the new look skirt was dictated in order to prevent it getting tangled up with the wheels. The slipper shoe was created for footplate comfort. The turtleneck sweater and the neckerchief were designed against draughts down the neck. . . By such means as this was the Italian girl's appearance transformed, and her emancipation consummated."*

— *"A New Race of Girls"* Picture Post
*September 5, 1954*

revolution, and they refrained from sponsoring scooter outings in the U.K. "The words 'social scootering' had formerly summoned up the image of orderly mass rallies. Now it was suddenly linked to a more sinister collective: an army of youth, ostensibly conformist—barely distinguishable as individuals from each other or the crowd—and yet capable of concerted acts of vandalism," according to Dick Hebdige in *Hiding in the Light.*

Meanwhile, the Mods would secretly plot the next seaside tiff—whether at Hastings or Clacton—and Scotland Yard would try to guess the Mods' move and fly in to quell the riot.

### SECOND AND THIRD MOD MOVEMENTS

Some social historians mourned the "death" of the Mods in the 1970s, like Dick Hebdige: "Somewhere on the way home from school or work, the Mods went 'missing.' They were absorbed into a 'noonday underground' of cellar clubs, discotheques, boutiques and record shops which lay hidden beneath the 'straight world.'" If only he would have

Black and white checks recall the Ska records of the Specials, Selector, and English Beat on this P-series Vespa. The lucky dice rolling craps keep the evil eye at bay.

Even the tail light of this two-tone Vespa 150 Super gets decked out with a customizing touch.

What's a scooter without accessories? Chrome crash bars guard the front fender of this Vespa from the inevitable dings and scratches of road racing.

searched a little harder, he would have found the Mod chameleon had just moved on to the next style.

In the 1970s, The Who's reenactment of the infamous Mod-Rocker wars in *Quadrophenia* rang true to a new generation when Jimmy uttered in his heavy Cockney about the motorcycling rebels, "All that greasy hair and dirty clothes. It's diabolical . . . I don't wanna be the same as everybody else. That's why I'm a Mod, see?"

This new wave rejected once-Mod bands like The Rolling Stones, The Kinks, and even The Who as greasy Rockers, and instead latched on to a music style imported from Jamaica when young British holiday goers came back from the Caribbean inspired by Ska and Dub Reggae of bands like the Skatalites.

Soon Brit bands like Selector, The Specials, The English Beat, and Madness filled dancehalls with the quick treble guitar strummed on the upbeat and Hammond organs plunking out the melody.

"Two-tone" came to be the ultimate Mod description since it described the checkered patterns of clothes, two-tone scooters, the legendary record label releasing the best Ska, and the idea of black and white, Jamaican and British, coming together to produce the best music of the late seventies and eighties.

While most new-wave Mods just wanted to shake their booty to Ska, some

## HABERDASHER HAPPINESS: SAN-FRAN-STYLE MOD
### JONATHAN OGILVY

The first ride I took on my first Vespa was to the Salvation Army to find an outfit to help me look the part. This was 1984. The overwhelming majority of local Vespisti at that time were quick to help me by telling me what was wrong with my look. That is perhaps a clue to why so few scooterists dress in sharp suits anymore. Nevertheless, I appreciated the many pointers along the way to haberdasher happiness. Today, in case there may be one young master of his own destiny interested in a fresh start, I offer a primer. Of course the variations never end, and, as anyone will tell you, you have to redefine it for yourself. As Charles Mingus said, "You have to improvise on something," so here is a basic 'see sharp' scale.

•**Jacket.** Part of the fun of finding things in thrift stores is that they don't have to fit the way a tailor would want them to. You'll be hard pressed to find a tailor who will submit to making a jacket too small for you, and if you do find one, you'll still feel weird about paying him for it. This isn't to say finding a barrel-chested lad's castoffs is any easier. It may be a matter of finding something that fits you close but not tight around the middle and having it shortened by a bewildered old man who will be glad to get any kind of business in the current climate of new bohemians in New York and slobs in Hollywood.

•**Tie.** The tie is what brings the whole ensemble together. If you're not sure how to achieve this effect you can blow the whole thing apart so, in such cases, it is better to wear an open neck. Only practice will give you a confident half-Windsor, anyway, though we are working with the one- to two-inch-wide variety here, which is easier for getting symmetrical half knots and, for that matter, small full knots. Only practice, for that matter, will keep your tie out of your drink and out of your dirty motor oil.

Note: Only a professional comedian ever wears a tie with a polo neck and even then it is sometimes more painful to behold than it is hilarious.

•**Coat.** Not only does riding a scooter allow you to wear a full-length coat, the weather sometimes necessitates it. On the occasions when you don't have to worry about rain puddling in your groin area, but you do have wind, a three-quarter-length coat is nice to have. J and J Crombie of Leeds started making such coats in 1805 and they're pretty good at it by now. If you happen upon a genuine Crombie coat, well, lucky you. It is possible, however, to find such coats made by imitators, cheap and spendy alike, much to your satisfaction.

•**Shoes.** Paul Weller wore a kitchen apron onstage. Maybe it was to protect his suit from his guitar. Maybe it was because aprons are cool. He also sported sandals now and then, a far cry from his two-tone brogues and bicycle-striped bowling shoes. Now, unless you have the pull to go around in an apron and get away with it, don't wear sandals to ride a scooter. Desert boots are plenty comfortable. If you're going dancing, try something Italian with leather soles.

•**Socks.** When sitting on a scooter, your socks show. London faces of 1959 favored electric-blue nylon, what Stateside shoe shiners call "pimp socks."

Especially when everything else about your getup is downplayed, play up what gets hidden. This trick has been perfected by distinguished men from mainland China. It doesn't mean you're a homosexual. It means you have both sophistication and a sense of humor. Try not to steal your girlfriend's socks. Try to have socks she will steal from you.

•**Trousers.** Tapered to 14 1/2 inches is fine. Some guys like 'em so tight they can barely get their foot through and that makes some sense when it comes to keeping the wind out on the high road, but 14-inch hems work reasonably well. Cuffs and pleats are unnecessary and unwanted. Keep it streamlined. Try on a pair of razor-creased flat-fronted trousers and watch your speedometer to see how much faster you go.

•**Belt.** Keep it short. It's hard, when you can scoot from door to door, to remember to exercise. If you're not careful you'll soon be driving one of those Floridian sidewalk scooters. Let's say you're just fat, though, no matter how much exercise you get and how little beer you drink. Charles Mingus may have looked ridiculous riding a little fold-up bicycle around Greenwich Village, being a big man, but in no way did he look ridiculous in a 1962-style suit. No excuses, then, for letting everything go. Wear it with pride, thanks to a good tailor.

•**Shirt.** When holding the handlebars, one's cuffs show. Don't go crazy over cufflinks though. French cuffs do not go with button-down collars, which are preferred, especially with little colored buttons that will show on one's cuffs as well. Short sleeves and polo necks . . . okay, I don't know any rules about those. I suppose practical sport shirts are part of the fact that none of this needs to be exceedingly difficult. Who's going to wear a custom-made shirt every day?

Now, no one is telling you can't cover up jeans and a T-shirt in a big army parka. In fact I have known some damn smart dressing dudes to rock that very look with aplomb, no socks in the loafers even. The audacity! It doesn't matter. It was John Coltrane (who had but one suit, with spare "fat" pants) who said, "When you know the notes to sing, you can sing most anything." —Jonathan Ogilvy

*"The scooter is a device that we refuse to grace with a description of a motor cycle and which, therefore, has no place in this work."*
—Richard Hough in his snobby introduction *to* A History of the World's Motor Cycles.

**Decked out in Ducati leathers, this storm trooper is ready to take on the competition on the A1 autostrada or the *pista* at Monza.**

tried to get philosophical, like the 1980s 'zine *Absolute Beginners*: "MOD, MODERN. It means now, here, us. It means motion. Moving towards the future .... To live with style and hope. That is the human spirit which powers Mods like electricity through wires."

In 1995, *The Independent* declared that "This is the third British mod wave," when a Mod revival hit the runways from Milan to London. Fashion designer Anna Sui placed Linda Evangelista on a vintage Lambretta and pushed her out onto the runway (as if this was something revolutionary). A 1995 *Vogue* article, however, raved and quoted Anna Sui's futurist philosophy, "I looked at early-eighties mod like the Jam and current bands like Elastica,

then mixed all three decades up to make it more *today*."

In spite of what fickle designers say is "in" this minute, Mod style and music has never been so widespread with more Ska bands than ever before (from Let's Go Bowling to The Mighty, Mighty Bosstones), and even making a transformation into Lounge culture with the revival of cheesy big band players like Esquivel. More than anything, Mod is a state of mind, to be willing to advance into the future rather than bask in nostalgia.

## VESPA BOUTIQUES: FROM CUFFLINKS TO BATH SALTS

The Vespa first came to the United States in force via Sears department stores right next

When Corradino d'Ascanio developed the first Vespa, he envisioned a step-through vehicle for women in dresses with a covered motor to avoid engine grime. Women's emancipation rode on two wheels through the cobblestone piazzas of Italy and the *ragazzo*—even if he has tattooes—is relegated to the pillion.

*"Thus pills medically prescribed for the treatment of neuroses were used as ends-in-themselves, and the motor scooter, originally an ultra-respectable means of transport, was turned into a menacing symbol of group solidarity."*

—*Dick Hebdige in* Subculture

To avoid bothersome burns or feet trapped in the spokes, pillion passengers should try to keep their feet on the floorboards. A passenger may almost double the weight of the bike, so leaning too hard or working against the driver can cause spills.

to the lawn mowers and washing machines. Imports were halted in 1984 when Vespa couldn't meet U.S. emission standards and Piaggio was worried about product liability laws. The remaining scooters were resuscitated by devoted mechanics working for peanuts to keep these Italian marvels alive.

New Vespas are now back in the United States with a sleek new design, while the basic shape remains the same. These new versions of the classic have appeared in any number of TV ads, and were even featured on *Good Morning America*—although Diane Sawyer didn't do much for scooterists' inferi-

ority complex when she hopped on a Vespa exclaiming, "We're not Hell's Angels, we're hell's dorks!" Even so, big stars like Jay Leno, Sandra Bullock, and Robert DeNiro have all splurged for a new Vespa.

The classy new scooters are sleek, modern versions of the classic without all the vibrations and front-brake dipping which made the Vespa infamous. They tote a hefty price tag, however, which takes into account these updates. "If you don't care about quality or image, buy a plastic Yahama scooter. If you want to buy into the Vespa lifestyle, we're the place," said Jim D'Aquila, the co-owner of the Vespa Boutique in downtown Minneapolis, in 2002.

What's that? Did you say "Boutique"? The unfortunate moniker does little to

Even the Harley crew can appreciate Suzuki's Burgman with its enormous 632cc engine. The motorcycle-cum-scooter has been dubbed a "maxiscooter" and rarely makes appearances at scooter meets, but has been spotted on the streets of Sturgis. What's more, you don't have the raucous thumping noise of a Harley panhead to wake up the neighbors.

Yamaha's Zuma bucked the trend of the usual sport bikes and gave itself a distinct design—even if the dual headlamps are a tip of the hat to Ducati.

Yamaha's Vino is the perfect accessory for the fashion minded while zipping to a business meeting on Madison Avenue or the latest John Waters musical on Broadway. Scooters' step-through design make mounting the little beast easier than straddling a hefty motorcycle.

*"[The Mods] began by experimenting with purple hearts and other pep-pills, then progress via 'reefers' (marijuana) to heroin and cocaine—the two drugs that almost always lead to death before the age of thirty-five."*

—Sunday Mirror *in 1964*

dispel the "Italian hairdryer" myth, but seems to fit the new digs. Where else can you find Vespa watches, Vespa silver cufflinks, Vespa perfume, Vespa bath foams, Vespa herbal cream, Vespa bath oil, Vespa bath salts (in strawberry, mint, musk, and rose scents)?

Hard-core scooterists, on the other hand, are willing to get a little grease under their fingernails, such as Jeremy Liebig who fixes up old Vespas at his Scooter Lab garage and refused an offer to work for the new store.

*Minnesota Motorcycle Monthly*'s scooter columnist Jeremy Wilker referred to the Vespa store as "the Gap approach," since dozens of such boutiques opened around the country.

With Vespa clones such as the Bajaj and Stella giving Piaggio stiff competi-

tion, ironically by using its own classic design, the new Vespa war will be waged in the showrooms and on the streets. The Vespa Boutique owners in Minneapolis remained confident of the outcome. When I asked co-owner Gary Kiese some details about the new Vespas, however, he told me, "I can answer any questions you have on Ducatis and other Italian motorcycles." Could it be that the Rockers have won after all?

As of 2005, many of the upscale Vespa boutiques have shut their doors after being unable to keep up the necessary sales quotas. Nevertheless, Piaggio continues to sell its scooter in most major metropolitan areas in the United States, and Vespa's reentry into the United States can be credited with spurring a new scooter craze on Main Street USA.

"My other vehicle is a Mercedes," according to the reflection in the side panel of this Yamaha Vino 125.

The urge to modify your Vespa surges within every scooterist. While car owners are strangely conservative in preserving the factory finish—with the notable exception of art cars and dragsters—scooterists view their side panels and legshield as a canvas to make their ride their own.

*"We will fight them on the beach!"*
—*Churchill-mocking rallying cry of hyped-up Mods ready to battle the Rockers in Brighton*

# TOURS AND RALLIES

Chapter 6

## WHAT YOU WILL LEARN

- The origin of scooter obstacle courses called "Gymkhana"
- How to plan a rally and get the most bang for your buck
- That Vespa's designer envisioned scooter rallies on the moon
- That Julius Caesar's crossing the English Channel was later achieved by a Vespa
- How two French legionnaires went AWOL from Vietnam via Vespa
- That the Italian military planned a blitzkrieg regiment of Vespa Armed Forces

*Gone Fishin'*
**Just pop the Johnson Sea Horse on the back of the Cushman next to the tacklebox and head to the lake. Rather than bake in an oven-like large automobile—or "Sardine Mobile" as Vespa ads called them—smart scooterists enjoyed the natural air-conditioning of wind to keep their heads cool and their hair blow-dried.**

A scooter is a social appliance. While automobiles shield people from the outside world, putt-putts open up new horizons with new people to meet. Just add a Vespa and soon piazzas and coffee shops are buzzing with scooterists. As the *New Yorker* warned in 1957, "This is more than a fad, it's a revolution, and I don't see how anything can stop it."

Romance on two wheels springs eternal as scooterists are dying to meet and find a mate for the pillion. "Sports riders in this country are mostly either single or newly marrieds (scooters are so conducive to romance that there is a fast turnover between these categories)," according to a 1957 *Popular Science* article.

Social scooter protocol is strict. "It's an unwritten code for scooterists to greet each other," said a Vespa rider in the *New York Times Magazine* in 1958. If a scooterist sees a broken-down putt-putt on the side of the road, etiquette requires assistance even if the

driver has never even looked under the side panels before.

Laws that rule motorcycles are inevitably applied towards scooterists who try to show that they aren't the "Wild Ones." The *New York Times Magazine* backed them up in 1957 claiming that "Scooterists emphasize that they drive for pleasure, not for speed." The *New Yorker* as well defended the straight-laced scooterists as "an increasing number of quietly dressed, sober-looking scooterists of both sexes and a variety of ages darting amiably, by day and night, through the thick of midtown traffic."

Since scooters broke the ice between riders, groups met to discuss their raison d'être. "What are the club's purposes?" a scooterist demanded in a 1956 *New Yorker* article. "Thinking up scooter trips, getting discounts on spare parts, lobbying for the abolition of such laws as the one that keeps us off parkways."

Today many of these scooter clubs in

◀ **114** ▶

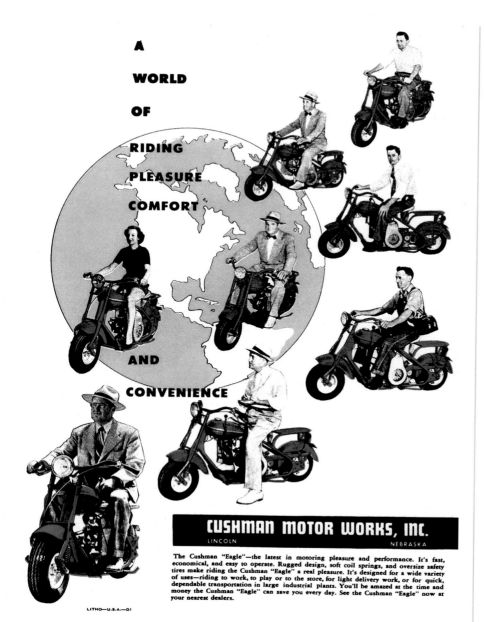

A WORLD OF RIDING PLEASURE COMFORT AND CONVENIENCE

## CUSHMAN MOTOR WORKS, INC.
LINCOLN                                                    NEBRASKA

The Cushman "Eagle"—the latest in motoring pleasure and performance. It's fast, economical, and easy to operate. Rugged design, soft coil springs, and oversize safety tires make riding the Cushman "Eagle" a real pleasure. It's designed for a wide variety of uses—riding to work, to play or to the store, for light delivery work, or for quick, dependable transportation in large industrial plants. You'll be amazed at the time and money the Cushman "Eagle" can save you every day. See the Cushman "Eagle" now at your nearest dealers.

LITHO—U.S.A.—D!

*"The Vespa is the world's greatest urban vehicle . . . its natural home is the city. New York, like Rome, needs to be lived on foot to appreciate its infinite mystery—not by subway or taxi car. But you'll see more of its mystery if you can be motored around it in the open air."*

—author Bill Buford

Europe have new, younger members, and America has seen dozens of clubs spring up, thanks in part to the recent return of classic-styled bikes and hours spent by the scooter loyalists restoring their vintage steed.

## GYMKHANA COURSES

Scooter obstacle courses are mandatory at any scooter rally to test the members' agility around blaze-orange cones, over wooden teeter-totters, and off jumps. "Gymkhana" courses prove riding ability and give scooterists a chance to show how slow they can go. A 1959 Cushman comic delved into Gymkhana's origin: "Historians believe the British started them in India. Mounted

horsemen of the Bengal Lancers sharpened battle maneuvers by wheeling and turning through obstacles." This was true inspiration to hop on a Cushman and practice war maneuvers, or imagine fighting Bengal tigers atop a two-stroke.

By the time Cushman plotted how to set up a Gymkhana course, scooter sports had already been played for a couple of decades, including tippy putt-putt polo. According to *Popular Mechanics* in 1939, "A bit faster than bicycle polo, the motorized sport brings occasional spectacular spills, but it's easy to jump off and the injuries to players are few," (but dramatic). Perhaps not aware of the earlier article,

*Popular Mechanics* once again announced the dawn of this new sport in 1947, "Scooters have invaded the sporting world and 'scooter polo' has been played as a stunt to large crowds."

## SCOOTER RAIDS

The newfound freedom that comes with two wheels urged scooterists off of the obstacle courses and instead to climb mountains, traverse continents, and attach pontoons to a putt-putts to cross the English Channel. Putting scooters to cross-country endurance tests were called "raids," and naturally were splendid publicity for scooter makers when news spread that a Vespa climbed Snowdon, that a group of Lambrettas went from London to Milan *nonstop*, or that

**Vespa auf Deutschland**
Perhaps more than any other country, Germany embraced scooters as the perfect medium to get away on vacation. Two German companies—Hoffmann and Messerschmitt—traded off producing Vespas when the scooters weren't imported directly from Italy. *Kruger Archives*

**"Happiness Goes with Lambretta"**
Innocenti's Lambretta offered 125cc power and a second seat from the beginning, marking it as the social scooter over the Vespa's single-seat, bare-bones functionality. The Lambretta was ideal for courting and cruising the piazza, as scooters opened Italian horizons postwar, giving mobility to youngsters and spreading youth culture far and wide. In the 1940s, the woman rode on the motorcycle pillion seat, sitting side-saddle as a lady should. That was all about to change forever, in a large part due to the motorscooter.

## WORDS TO THE WISE: PLANNING A TOUR

•**Gas stops.** If you're going to travel far out of town, make sure you've considered how far you can make it on a tank of gas and when you'll fill up. Very small towns may not even have gas stations. If they do, don't expect them to be open on Sundays or around the clock.

•**Tires.** Don't leave town on bare tires, and bring a spare.

•**Mechanicals.** Before you leave, make sure that you have plenty of oil (or have just changed it). Go around your scooter with a wrench and tighten every loose nut and bolt. These can rattle free when on the road, especially if your bushings are older. Double-check your shocks, coolant (if applicable), and battery fluid.

•**Spare parts and a tool kit.** (see the section on what to carry in your glovebox)

•**Water.** Keep hydrated on the road because your sweat may evaporate faster than you realize. Fill that water bottle full at every stop.

•**First aid kit.** Besides any prescription medicine you need, pack a bee sting or snake bite kit. Bring a little package of bandages, gauze with some tape, and alcohol or other antibiotic.

•**Camera.** Your trip is an adventure, after all, and you want to share it with friends back home. If your camera is valuable, wrap it in plastic. Keep it handy and not buried in a bag so you can get a close-up of that moose chasing you down the road.

•**Maps.** Plot your course carefully. Are there any long stretches between towns? Check with the highway department to see if any road construction will block your path. Do you have to drive on any freeways?

•**Cell phone.** Once a luxury, now a necessity in case of an accident. If you don't have one, most drivers carry one and will help if you're in a pinch. Don't expect to get cell phone reception if you're off the beaten track.

•**Rain gear.** If it starts to rain, the best plan is to pull over at a nice restaurant and wait it out. Unfortunately, the perfect place to stop rarely presents itself. While scooters are made to keep water from splashing on you, the top of your body will still get wet (unless you're driving one of those slick, covered BMW scooters).

•**Clothes.** Bring only the bare necessities, but always bring enough to make your trip comfortable. Don't expect a clean change of clothes each day, unless you plan on toting a trailer behind you. Remember that the temperature suddenly feels cooler when you're riding.

•**Storage.** Classic scooters were designed for tooling around town, not for long distance drives. Intrepid scooterists didn't listen to the designers and concocted storage systems devised from milk crates, bungee cords, and gunny sacks. Avoid backpacks as this will limit your ability to react while on your scooter, and the weight will tire your shoulders after carrying the pack all day. The good news is that modern scooters come with much more storage, and dealers usually offer extra storage compartments (for an extra price) that blend into your scooter's design. Numerous aftermarket storage systems are available but can sometimes be a chore to mount on your bike. Two of the standbys for classic scooters are: Scooterworks in Chicago (www.scooterworks.com) and West Coast Lambretta Works (www.lambretta.net). If you don't want to invest in a hard shell compartment (which are nice to keep the rain out), consider securing your pack to your rack with a bungee net.

•**Plastic bags.** Wrap your clothes in plastic bags, even if they're inside a supposedly waterproof sack. If the rain comes down hard you'll be happy to have warm, dry clothes at the end of a long day's ride.

While scooters were initially envisioned as a two-wheeled folks-mobile to mobilize the masses and ensure a burgeoning economy, the peppy two-strokes proved to be the ideal machine for zipping around on vacation, especially along the sunny French Riviera.

*"The scooter serves as the material bridge between different generations, different cultures, different epochs, between contradictory desires. It is a sign of progress.... It is a passport to the future."*
—Dick Hebdige in "Object as Image: The Italian Scooter Cycle"

### Beautiful Sundays

Piaggio followed Innocenti's lead and plopped a second seat on the back of its Vespa and tuned up the engine with enough oomph to carry a passenger. Just as Coco Chanel shocked French culture with her decadent designs, scooters freed women from rigid French culture of proper pinky-in-the-air protocol and put them in the driver's seat. Crank that transistor radio and munch that apple of love. Society would never be the same again.

### Bellicose Bernadet

Just as the ACMA Vespa was armed with a bazooka by the French foreign legion to fight (unsuccessfully) the uprising in Algeria, France's finest attempted another scooter experiment by pulling artillery with a home-grown Bernadet. *François-Marie Dumas archives*

### Scooters Florentine

High above the hills of Florence, scooterists from Naples, Lucca, and Cesena consult near the Boboli Gardens before continuing on their raid through the Tuscan hills. Perhaps these Italian scooterists feared falling into the white rabbit's hole outside Florence that led Dante Alighieri to the many levels of Inferno.

# Cushman Airborne Scooter
MODEL 53 A

## NOW Available for Civilian Use

**A**T LAST a closely guarded war secret can be told. During the preparation of the American Forces for the invasion of Germany, we were called upon to design a special Cushman Motor Scooter for the United States Army Paratroopers and since our victory in Germany, this very important piece of war transportation is available for civilian use.

We are proud to present this Model "53A" Airborne Motor Scooter to the American public for their use in safe, economical and enjoyable transportation.

This Airborne Scooter was designed and built to withstand the rigors of war. To this sturdiness has been added all the features of our regular scooter to assure you of an easy, comfortable ride.

The picture above illustrates how the Cushman Airborne Scooters are dropped by parachute from planes in the sky to give the paratroopers extra maneuverability on the ground.

The "Airborne" scooter was designed and built sturdy enough to withstand the severe shock and jolt in landing. Powered by the famous "Husky" engine, this machine travels over all kinds of terrain, through mud, sand, up steep inclines and even through underbrush. It has met the rigorous tests of war and earned an enviable record for speedy, dependable transportation at an amazingly low cost.

IN THE CITY

ON THE FARM

## CUSHMAN MOTOR WORKS
Lincoln 1, Nebraska

---

## A SUCCESSFUL RIDE:
### NERDY ADVICE TO HAVE A SAFE "SNAKE" OF SCOOTERS

Riding en masse requires a group-think of scooterists to form as one line, or snake, slithering up switchbacks along mountain passes or stopping traffic down Broadway. Here are some basic rules of the road for each rider to adhere to and become one with the gang.

- Stop for gas before setting out.
- Be certain everyone knows the course in case someone gets separated.
- Don't plan a ride that is too long for most scooterists to handle, especially if some of the bikes are classics.
- Ask to see if everyone's bike is legal (license, insurance) because cops love to pull over scooters.
- Bring extra cables.
- For longer rides, have someone drive a pickup or a van along in case of breakdowns.
- If riding through stoplights, make sure the lead people slow down or wait.
- Try to ride in formation (two by two)—but only at slower speed and if scooterists know how to do it.
- Save popping wheelies and burning rubber for the Gymkhana course.

---

Vespisti braved the cold in a raid to the Arctic Circle.

Innocenti realized that loyal Lambrettisti traveling the globe would do more to promote their scooters than advertising ever could. Scooters became a way to unite the world—whether a Wall Street businessman or an Albanian partisan, everyone could appreciate the convenience and freedom given by these little two-strokes. Scooterists on raids became missionaries, with their angelic wings being a flashy Lambretta and pillion seat as two tickets to paradise.

A 1950s Innocenti advertising campaign called "The Whole World of Lambretta" tried to break down national boundaries, making the scooter the ultimate unifier as it "showed scooters posed against Buddhist temples or busy London streets," according to Dick Hebdige. Innocenti showed this again in a 1954 advertising film, *Travel Far, Travel Wide*, "A frontier. And on the other side, a completely different way of life. But whatever country you go to in the world today, you'll find Lambrettas and Lambretta service stations."

The Lambretta Club of Great Britain led annual "Scooter Tours" to Germany, Switzerland, and Austria to spread the word about Lambrettas, and even "Italy in

## PLANNING THE RALLY

### •Getting the Word Out

Most people who show up at your rally will hear about it via other scooterists. See if someone in your scooter gang is an artist or designer and will make a logo for the rally. Using the design, print up posters to tack up in bars, cafés, and, of course, scooter shops.

Make a small version of the poster and copy it on cardstock for postcards. Leave small stacks at the scooter shop and send them out to your fellow scooteristi.

Create a website using a scan of the logo and announce your event to the world. If you don't know how to make a website, someone in your scooter club will surely be able to help. Extras on the website should include a chatroom, a place to list scooters and parts for sale, and links to scooter shops and mechanics. Make sure that interested scooterists can leave their e-mail addresses with you so you can tell them about future rallies.

### • Call the Media

Send a press release (essentially just an announcement) about the event to the daily newspaper, the weekly papers, the monthly magazines, and even TV and radio. If you don't feel like writing up a separate press release, just send them a postcard or an e-mail.

Give yourself plenty of time, weeks if not months, to organize the event and tell the media as soon as possible. If you send an announcement a week before the rally, some newspapers may be able to squeeze a listing of the event into their pages. If you warn them a month ahead of time, they may assign a writer and photographer to run a feature article on your rally.

### • Call the Cops

The chances are you won't need any sort of "parade" license for your rally. However, if you roll out on the streets with a hundred scooters, cops just love to check that everything is in order.

It doesn't hurt to call the local precinct and ask them if you need any sort of permit to have a scooter ride. Be prepared to give the course that you are planning on following with your group. If the police say it should be fine, get a name of someone there who gave you permission. If your rally is stopped by the cops, at least you can pull out the name of someone at the local precinct who gave you the OK.

### • Plotting the Course

Show off your city's best. Plan a trip around the lakes, along the river, by the seaside, through the hills, by the waterfalls. Drive down Main Street as if you're on parade. Meet at a favorite café to load up on coffee or another place where people won't mind hanging out for a bit to wait for the stragglers (plan to leave on time, but expect to leave a little late). Plan the route to have a gas station near the beginning. Even if you tell everyone to fill up, inevitably a few forget. At the end of the ride, be sure that scooterists can quench their thirst and grab a bite to eat.

If you have a large group of scooterists, consider splitting up into two rides—one long, one short. This way, scooterists with fragile classics won't worry about breaking down on a short ride and speedsters won't complain about a short trip.

### • Draw Maps

Make sure that at least two scooterists know the route. Put one in front and the other in the rear in case the group is separated. Before setting out on your snake of scooters, describe the path you'll follow to the group. Ideally, draw a map with familiar landmarks or sites to see along the way. Internet mapping programs such as MapQuest can help if drawing isn't your forte.

### • Pre-Riding

Before committing to a certain itinerary for the trip, hop on your scooter and ride the route. This is the only way you'll notice certain hazards that may require a detour. No scooters will want to go en masse on the interstate, over dirt roads, or by a sewage treatment plant. To prevent a snake of two hundred scooters running into road construction, ride the route a day or two before the big event.

### • Warn the Venue

Before a hundred scooters roll into the parking lot of your favorite bowling alley or coffee shop for your town's biggest rally ever, give the venue a heads up. Almost any restaurant or café would love to fill their booths with hungry and thirsty scooterists, but they'll be far more appreciative if they know you're coming. Who knows? A few employees could be gaga for scooters and will help convince the owner to spread out the red carpet for your line of putt-putts. If you do get coverage of the rally in the newspaper before the event, imagine the surprise of the venue's owners if they see they are hosting a rally and they had no idea.

### • Sponsors

Call up your local scooter shop and see if they'll sponsor your rally. Sometimes the shop will help with a small donation to offset printing costs or other expenses. Often, the scooter shop will agree to host the event at their store in an attempt to lure in customers. Depending on the nature of the scooter shop, this can also change the feel of the rally to be more of a commercial ploy than a fun ride.

If you're planning a picnic, hit up the local grocery store or co-op to see if they'll donate some food. Ask the local independent record store or bookshop to donate a few gift certificates for door prizes. Sometimes generous scooter makers will donate a scooter to be given away at a raffle. You'll be surprised at how generous stores will be and you won't know until you ask. In return, you'll put their logo on all your fliers, website, and maybe T-shirts for the event. Sponsors also expect that it will be a decent-sized rally if they're going to donate.

## TIME CAPSULE

### SCOOTS ON THE MOON:
### LUNAR LANDING

In 1976, just seven years after Neil Armstrong stepped on the earth's moon, Vespa designer Corradino D'Ascanio predicted his scooter would someday conquer space. In an interview on Italian television, he bragged about the timelessness of his design by saying, "The Vespa will always look like it does, even when it is powered by a mini nuclear reactor or as a vehicle to drive on the moon."

Britain" was proclaimed for the annual National Lambretta Club annual rally held in the U.K.

The scooter that went around the world—easily beating Magellan's record—

was a 1954 Mustang. American Dick Miller circumvented the globe armed only with extra inner tubes, fuel tanks, an American flag, and "USA" written everywhere on his

### *Veni, Vidi, Vespa*
**For the 1960 Olympics in Rome, Piaggio helped equip a fleet of Vespas for the Olympic Village. Just as Charlton Heston drove a Vespa after his famous chariot scene in *Ben Hur*, so did the Olympians hop on a scooter after the Roman games.**

### *Piaggio Factory*
**While the entrance to the famous Piaggio factory in Pontedera near Pisa may not seem like more than a dingy gray arch in typical fascistic architectural chest-thumping style, the genius within those gates, however, has put Italy and the world on two wheels. "*Scusi signore. Non si può fare fotografie dentro!*" warns a security guard who switches to his pidgin English, "No photo! No photo!"**

**Dueling Lambrettas**
In the central Norwegian town of Trondheim, Ralph Henriksen and Steinar Nesje risk parking tickets from the *norsk politi* for leaving their vintage Lambrettas on this downtown walking street. The Trondheim Omeng Scooter Klubb abbreviates to "T.O.S.K.," Norwegian slang for fool. Thankfully, these Nordic scooterists don't take themselves too seriously, but still manage to run a snake of classic scooters over the mountain pass into Sweden on a pleasure trip.

**Raid to the English Lakes**
This chap—along with a larger contingent of Lambretta LDs—took snapshots every step of their way through northern England. Innocenti, the company that made Lambrettas, thanked the scooter god that these little two-wheelers didn't require situating the steering wheel on the opposite side for British sales.

scooter. The scooter shrunk distances and brought people together around the world.

## SIDE CARS:
## BRING THE WHOLE FAMILY

Scooter engines struggled when a passenger was plopped on the pillion. Even so, a *seitenwagen* was often attached to the frame to bring the whole household along. Imaginative designs of a shoemaker's sidecar as a huge loafer and a baker's delivery mobile in the shape of a loaf of bread were welded as a third wheel to scooter frames. Even during the war, "...sidecars were added to convert them into mobile soda fountains for carrying refreshments to production-line workers. Other sidecar combinations were equipped for ambulance duty and fire-fighting," according to *Popular Mechanics* in 1947.

Scooter manufacturers soon caught on to the idea of it as a stepping stone to a full-fledged automobile, and the microcar was born. Iso of Milano designed the famous Isetta front-opening mini-car later picked up by BMW; Piaggio's three-wheeled Ape Car is the preferred form of travel in Sicily and India; and Messerschmitt built the fantastic three- and four-wheeled KR200 looking like a pilot's cockpit and inspiring the sci-fi film *Brazil*.

## AQUATIC SCOOTERS:
### CALAIS TO DOVER VIA VESPA

Before Jet Skis, Georges "Jojo" Monneret was fed up with the ferry to get to Britain. Instead, he hooked up his 125-cc Vespa to a pair of pontoons with a glorified bathtub in between that held his scooter upright. The pokey Vespa engine powered a little two-blade propeller as he recreated a miniature version of William the Conqueror's and Julius Caesar's invasion of England. His first attempt was foiled, however, when he ran into a deviant tree stump floating in the drink. Back on French soil, he re-rigged his makeshift bateau with a three-blade prop and successfully crossed "La Manche" in 5 1/2 hours—a record never beaten or even attempted by any other foolhardy scooterist.

## ACROSS ASIA ON TWO WHEELS:
### AWOL ON A VESPA

Fed up with France's debacle in Indochina, a French soldier, armed only with his Vespa, left his brothers in the foreign legion to continue their hopeless war on the Viet Minh without him. Through some of the most rugged terrain in the world, the soldier steered his Vespa home to France.

Piaggio was listening and soon Vespa "raids" and dangerous feats were making headlines across the world. Daniel Sauvage put 15,500 miles on his Vespa traveling around the Mediterranean with his wife on the pillion and wrote *Ma Vespa, Ma Femme et Moi* in 1956. Victor Englebert, a Belgian photographer, traveled from Brussels to Cape Town, South Africa, in 1957.

In spite of all the fuss made by the homesick gendarme soldier in Indochina, news must not have reached JFK at the White House. Soon, U.S. troops replaced the fed-up French in the southeast Asian quagmire. The Vietnamese, on the other hand, heard the story of the perky Vespa and to this day manufacture their own Piaggio knock-offs—allbeit with questionable mechanical parts.

**One of the more popular events at scooter rallies is the slow race. In this race the object is to ride your scooter slower than the other guy. Serious competitors lower the air pressure in their tires to help the scooter stay upright even when it is practically standing still. This sport requires a rider with the patience of a monument.**

Gymkhana courses can be very challenging tests of a rider's skill.

Anyone competing in a Gymkhana course event will subject his or her scooter to abuse. If you have a rare antique scooter for which spare parts aren't readily available, you might want to leave the competition to those less concerned with keeping their scoots pristine.

## VESPA ARMED FORCES: A DREAM FOILED!

Italian hoodlums could easily outrun the poor *Carabinieri* military policemen atop their rickety one-speed Bianchi bicycles. As the perennial butt of jokes about their dimwitted authority, the Carabinieri decided to fight back in 1949 with plans for a *Vespa Forze Armate* (Vespa Armed Forces) to round up the petty pickpockets ruining tourists' Roman holidays. Running interference would be a back-up squadron of three-wheeled Ape-cars from Piaggio to supply the pompous policemen

with superior firepower. Enrico Piaggio called the putt-putt squadron to a halt before the two-strokes could fight crime or attack on the battlefield. Frustrated with more than two years of futile discussions with the Italian Carabinieri and NATO, Enrico complained, "I am ever more convinced that the 'military' are not worth the time of day."

## VAGABONDS AND TOURISTS: GERMANS TRAVEL THE WORLD

Lured by earthly wanderlust, intrepid German travelers often opted for the *Strolch*, or "vagabond," a scooter made by Progress that echoed the ad campaign of fellow German company Heinkel with its scooter, the Tourist. With an unusual pivoting headlamp on the front apron, the Progress—with optional engines of 150 cc or 200 cc—was backed by ads of romantic getaways to the beach and mountains, not the confining walls of most European cities where they would probably be used most.

The Progress crossed the English Channel to be licensed to a British firm (after changing the Teutonic mouthful *Strolch* to the more patriotic sounding "Briton," "Anglian," and "Britannia"). Travel was all the rage at the 1955 Geneva show, where the Progress appeared as a set with a Strolch-emblemed Steib sidecar. A trailer was also optional for extended scooter tours, but the little engine probably couldn't wind up Alpine roads with a loaded sidecar as well.

Heinkel scooters, on the other hand, had their roots back in 1922 when Ernst Heinkel built war materials, especially airplane parts for the fatherland. During World War I and World War II, Heinkel gave the Allies reason to quiver with its huge bombers forcing blackouts across England. Postwar, the rubble of the factory was reduced to making scooters, but the four-stroke 1953 Heinkel Tourist 101 was nothing to scoff at. While Deutschland's world domination may have been snuffed, Heinkel scooters succeeded in exporting German tourists to all parts of the globe during its 12-year reign with some of the most powerful and reliable scooters ever seen.

## COMMUNIST SCOOTERS?
## THE CHINESE DRAGON
## SEIZES GERMAN TECHNOLOGY

Having been reduced to producing potato mashers in postwar Germany, Zündapp of Nürnberg scored when it made a knock-off of Italy's 125-cc Parilla Levriere. The 150-cc Bella was born, and for 11 years the Bella was produced with a larger 200-cc engine, and by 1959, the R204 Bella was judged "amongst the best scooters on the market" by *Motor Cycling* magazine.

Even faraway China noticed the German prowess. In 1985, Zündapp agreed to sell its remaining merchandise to the People's Republic of China. 1,500 Chinese comrades traveled overland in a freight train to Munich, loaded up all the machinery and remaining stock (for two weeks sleeping in the boxcars at night to save money), and headed back to Asia to set up shop.

**The more widely you publicize your rally, the better the turn out will be.**

**Sidecars on scooters can be fun and practical, but they change the riding dynamic completely and require a different set of skills to operate safely. Make certain you can control the rig before heading out into traffic.**

# CLUBS

## WHAT YOU WILL LEARN

- How to find the nearest scooter rally
- How to join your local scooter club
- Tips on how to form your own scooter club
- The tale of two cities and their scooters: Milan's Lambretta vs. Pisa's Vespa
- How the Masons ensured that scooters took over the world
- How women's liberation began with female scooter clubs

*Scooterists and Vespa in Traditional Costumes*
**Organizing the faithful into owners' clubs around the globe was one way to inspire loyalty to the cause, whether the cause is Vespa or Lambretta. Vespa clubs from around Europe gathered annually for the gigantic Eurovespa hoopla, also sponsored by Piaggio. At Eurovespa 1962, the Vespa Club de España dressed its members and its Spanish-made Vespas in traditional folk costumes to celebrate Spanish culture and Spanish scooter productivity.**

In 1951, Adolf Nass formed the first Vespa Club in Saarbrucken, Germany, just six years after the end of World War II, with dreams of a better world. His sense of Germanic organization led to the formation of more than 300 clubs. And thanks to Piaggio and 1,200 Vespa service stations around the world. Lambretta clubs formed as well, to show their loyalty to the scooter that gave them wings. *Vespa News*, *Lambretta Leader*, and *Jet-Set* were the newsletters translated into numerous languages for the loyal scooter legions.

## WOMEN'S CLUBS

After the scooter slump of the 1970s, women rediscovered the vehicle that was made with them in mind. Towards the end of the Mod revolution, female scooterists were fed up with being "pillion fodder," and sprang for a Lammie of their own. By the mid-1980s, the feminist press finally embraced the scooter as their ride. Writer Letty Cottin Pogrebin wrote in *Ms.* maga-

zine in 1987, "I discovered that the scooter provided a reliable litmus test of male character. Those who were threatened by it didn't last long in my affections."

Also in 1987, *Woman's Day* wrote an article about the thrill and freedom of scooter driving, paralleling a businessman becoming a weekend rebel on a Harley. "I'd never made a serious move about getting a scooter. I knew as well as anyone that cars come swinging around curves and there you are, tossed in the air like a matador on the horns of a bull." Even so, she couldn't resist the danger and told her readers to get a scooter of their own.

The scooter revival hit both haute couture and D.I.Y. punk scooterists. While *Vogue* ran a huge spread of "new" Vespa fashion, women-only scooter clubs popped up with names like "The Scheming Bitches Scooter Club" who declared, "We had a rule that our boyfriends couldn't drive our bikes with us on the back."

In 1997, *Scoot* magazine writer Christian Larsen profiled these new sororities. "Beware, fellow male Vespa and Lambretta riders, some of these girls will out-ride you, out-race you, out-fix you, and out-drink you." One of these dangerous dames of The Secret Servix Scootin' Chicks echoed the feminist cry to get off the pillion: "My favorite part of being a scooter girl is convincing those girls on the back of bikes to get their own."

## ANNUAL SCOOTER EVENTS

Each year, snakes of scooters climb mountains, ford rivers, and drive down Main Street. Rallies are held across the country with more and more members each year. Many motorcycle rallies (especially non-Harley events) welcome cool scooters to their shows.

For current listings of scooter events, check out: http://scoot.net/calendar/ or http://www.scooterworks.com/rssfeed.cfm

*"If you buy a Vespa, your neighbors don't move out of the neighborhood. The Vespa is a motorscooter, not a motorcycle. There is no social stigma attached to driving one."*
—Vespa ad from 1964

**Shriner Motor Corps**
The Motor Patrol from the Moslah Temple of Fort Worth, Texas, shows off their lineup of Cushman Super Eagles decked out in a dazzling array of special Shriner options. Cushman alone offered these accessories to Shriners on its scooters as well as the Vespas that Cushman began importing in 1961. Only later did other scooter and motorcycle makers such as Harley-Davidson or the American importers of BMW and Japanese machines jump on the bandwagon with Shriner accessories. *Courtesy Shriner Sam Nelson*

Moslah Temple Motor Corps
MOSLAH TEMPLE MOTOR CORPS
Organized March 1958

1. Director General Bob Lee, 2. B. Elston, 3. J. Norton, 4. A. Gray, 5. J. Ryfle, 6. E. Willms, 7. J. Sikes, 8. T. Atkins, 9. T. Brooks, 10. A. Bettis, 11. H. Milrany, 12. B. Stewart, 13. J. Nelson, 14. J. Brown, 15. G. Wilkinson, 16. M. Brown, 17. L. Brown, 18. L. Bolles, V. Woodard.

Here's a partial listing of some of the best scooter rallies:

• **Amerivespa** As an answer to Eurovespa, which has brought together hundreds if not thousands of Vespas from across that continent, Amerivespa was launched with the help of Piaggio and dedicated Vespisti in the U.S. This is now possibly the largest event in the country as other scooter groups are welcome to join. Amerivespa 2006 will be held in Denver. (http://www.amerivespa.org/)

**Vespa World Travelers**
Piaggio's German ads urged its riders to tour the globe by scooter and they'd find Vespa Service Stations in 120 countries eager to keep you zipping along. As the (alleged) most practical means of transportation in the world, the Vespa beats the camel, horse, elephant, or Cadillac any day. Never mind the stereotypes used to push the product. *Kruger Archives*

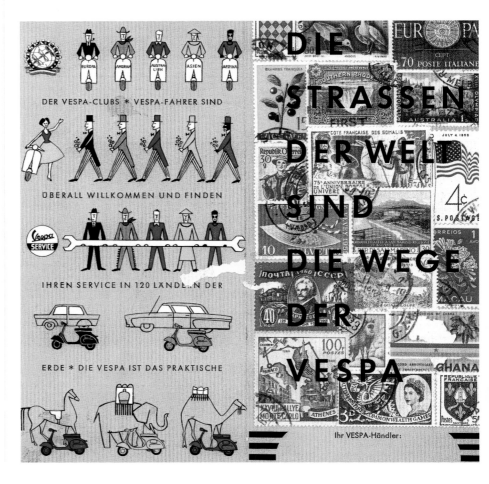

• **ASRA Races** American Scooter Racing Association (ASRA) sponsors tricked out scooter racing in California for those who lust speed. (http://www.scooterracing.info)

• **Bacchus Raucous** In honor of the Roman god of vino, the Bombastic Scooter Club sponsors this annual event in the Tri-Cities of Washington state. Be prepared to drink the sweet nectar of local wineries during the harvest time of late September. (http://www.bombasticsc.com)

• **Deliverance** The Imperial Scooter Club of Atlanta, Georgia, puts together this event just past the heat of the summer in mid-September. (http://forums.imperialsc.com/)

*"Despite modifications in design over the years, the overall conception and placement of the scooter—its project market, its general shape, its public image— remained fixed in the formula: motor cycles as men; scooters as women and children,"*
—Dick Hebdige in Object as Image: The Italian Scooter Cycle

• **Down N Dirty** The Jedi Knights Scooter Club sponsors this Halloween event in New Orleans, even after the floods! Now that's dedication. (http://www.jksc.org)

• **ESRA and MASS Scooter Races** The Eastern Scooter Racing Association and Mid America Scooter Sport host races in the summer in the Midwest and East Coast. (http://www.whizwheels.com/esra.html or http://sports.groups.yahoo.com/group/ESRA/)

• **Endless Summer** In a place like Santa Barbara they can scoot all year round and not worry about the weather. This event takes place in late September and is sponsored by the Vesparados. (http://www.vesparados.com)

• **Festering OktoberScoot** Before the rainy winter hits Seattle, Vespa Seattle sponsors this long-running event in late September. (http://www.drizzle.com/~vespaman or http://www.vespaseattle)

## SCOOTER CLUBS

In the past, most scooter clubs welcomed any kind of scooter from Vespa to Lambretta to Cushman. When someone showed up on a Harley Topper or Czechoslovakian Cezeta, club members gave standing ovations to this marvel of scooterdom. With the recent revival, however, many scooter clubs are brand specific or set guidelines that scooters must be "classic," "maxi," or some other limit.

Most scooter clubs don't charge a fee, so the benefits of joining don't include any sort of life insurance discount. Instead, members can swap knowledge, spare parts, and good stories. The culmination of scooter club membership usually results in an annual ride or participation in a larger regional ride.

The temporal nature of scooter clubs makes listing them a bit tricky. Web addresses change, club's names are updated, and members sell their scooters to move up to three-wheeled microcars. Here's an attempt to list (surely with gaps) some of the scooter clubs around the country.

**Cushman Club of America.** Often overlooked by modern scooter owners, the Cushman was the backbone of the American scooter revolution in the 1950s and 1960s. The club is still going strong with a huge annual meet and has entered the twenty-first century at http://www.hobbytech.com/CushmanClub.html.

**Honda Silver Wing Scooter Group.** This on-line club at http://autos.groups.yahoo.com/group/hondasilverwings/ meets over the internet to exchange information about the enormous Honda maxi-scooter, the Silver Wing.

Honda Reflex Owners Group Exchange spare parts, letters, and stories about the Reflex at http://autos.groups.yahoo.com/group/hondareflexowners/.

**Honda Helix Clubs.** As the first maxi-scooter to hit the road, the Honda Helix has the largest following. Honda Helix has its own web world at http://autos.groups.yahoo.com/group/hondahelixdiscussion/. Another interesting site is http://scootertrip.com/. And a group that meets for on-line chats about the Honda CN250 (Helix, Fusion) motorcycle is located at http://autos.groups.yahoo.com/group/cn250/.

**International Community of Burgman Owners.** These enormous maxiscooters have a dedicated following and this international club is accessible through http://www.burgmanusa.com/. Another on-line Suzuki Burgman club posts messages at http://autos.groups.yahoo.com/group/Suzuki_Burgman/.

**Lambretta Club of America.** Keeping those classic two-strokes alive and making even the Vespa look pokey, the Lambretta Club of America is a relatively new club that is also helping bring back the new Lambretta that everyone is waiting for. (http://www.lambretta.org/)

**Vespa Scooter Clubs.** Vespa clubs are by far the most organized of all scooter clubs. Some of them have the blessing of the parent company, Piaggio, but usually they operate independently and have kept the Vespa name alive, even when the company tried to retire it and released the "Cosa" scooter in its stead.

The parent Vespa club in the U.S. is located at http://www.vespaclubusa.org/. It can help you find the other smaller clubs in your area. The Vespa Club of America requires a membership fee, whereas many of the smaller clubs just want you to show up on your sparkling scooter.

**Proud of a Parilla**
The Moto Parilla Museum in Modigliana, Italy, may be comprised mostly of deathly fast racing bikes that tore up the track in the 1950s and 1960s, but a lone scooter stands proudly among these world class racers. And why not? The influential Parilla Levriere (or "greyhound" in English) was the basis for Sweden's Husqvarna, Germany's Victoria Peggy scooter, and the main influence behind Zündapp's first Bella.

• **Flagstaff Ride** High in the mountains of Arizona, these scooterists tune up their putt-putts for high altitude for the big ride in late September. (http://www.myspace.com/flagstaffride)

• **Freeze Your Balls Off Rally** Meeting in the depths of winter (usually January), this Durham, North Carolina, scooter club risks the snow of the southland. (http://www.series1studio.com/freezeyour ballsoff/)

• **Halifax Scooter Council Rally** This Canadian club is now in its seventh year of rallies that take place in Annapolis Royal, Nova Scotia. (http://www.halifaxscooter council.com)

• **High Rollers Weekend** This annual rally in Las Vegas features "fun in the sun and the sins of the night" in February. (http:// www.LVScooterRally.com)

• **High Rollers Weekend** Same name, different city. Taking place in early July in Montreal, this rally promises to be Canada's largest by drawing from American and European scooter clubs. Remember: "Even in French sin is still sin!"

• **Hurricane Run** The Vulcan Scooter Club sponsors this annual rally in early October just 90 miles from Cuba on beautiful Key West on the southernmost point in the U.S. (http://www.vulcansc.fr.st)

• **Independence Day Rally and Oktober Revolution** Sponsored by the Hostile City and Rabble Rouser Scooter Clubs of Philadelphia, the first annual rally takes place over the 4th of July weekend and the second one in the fall. (http://www.hostilecitysc.org or http://www.rabblerousersc.com)

• **Love 'Em & Leave 'Em** This all-girls rally takes place in balmy St. Augustine, Florida, in mid-October. (http://autos.groups.yahoo.com/group/girl sscooterrally/ or http://www.lambrettagirl.com/Rally)

**1949 Lambretta Racer**
Innocenti's battle axe was this racer built with at least the idea of the production Model B in the far back of someone's mind. Any parts the street scoot and this full-bore racer shared where purely by accident, but the name on the side of the gas tank was enough.

• **Lu'au-au-go-go** Who needs an excuse to zoom a scooter around Honolulu, Hawaii? This new event takes place in mid-October.

• **Mile-High Mayhem** This annual scooter rally in Denver, Colorado, has become one of the largest in the country.

• **Night of the Vespastics.** This pre-Halloween bash takes place in Los Angeles, San Francisco, and New Orleans. Or as they say, "One Night, Two Strokes, Three Cities." (http://www.vespastics.com)

• **PVSC City Rally** Pittsburgh Vintage Scooter Club sponsors this annual event at the beginning of October for one last ride before winter in the steel city. (http://www.steelcityscooters.com/)

• **Run from the Sun** Top Dead Center Scooter Club of Oregon plans this annual event drawing scooteristi from Portland and Eugene in mid-September. (http://www.topdeadcentersc.com)

• **Saints and Scooters** The Upstart Scooter Club organizes this annual rally through Salt Lake City in early September. (http://www.upstartsc.us)

• **Scoot-a-Que** The Columbus Cutters of Ohio plan this annual event for mid-September complete with a BBQ and gymkhana obstacle courses. (http://www.scootcolumbus.com)

• **Skooter Dü** Named for hometown rockers Hüsker Dü, Minneapolis' annual rally now tops 150 scooters at this summer event, in spite of winter clogging the roads for half the year. (http://www.minnescoota.com/skooterdu/)

• **Skutober Fest** The Secret Society Scooter Club of San Diego hosts this annual rally in conjunction with Scooters West. (http://www.Secretsociety.org)

• **SlaughterHouse** In honor of its town's fame as the center of the butchering biz, Chicago's Los Corazones Negros Scooter Club sponsors one of the largest Midwest rallies at the beginning of September, riding through the city with a good-and-dangerous gymkhana at the end. (www.slaughterhousechicago.com)

• **Southern Discomfort Rally** Sponsored by the Birmingham Scooter Syndicate, this annual rally runs through the streets of Alabama's capital in November. (http://www.birminghamscootersyndicate.com)

*"Every time I'm waiting at a traffic light, there is always at least one pedestrian who, rushing past me, does a doubletake. "Whoa, dude, Vespa!" he'll say (or some variation thereof). And he stops, right there in the middle of the street to admire what's between my legs."*
—*author Bill Bulford*

*Ready to Race*
Through rain, sleet, or packs of
Lambrettas, this Vespa driver was ready
for an endurance race sponsored by the
local French Vespa club in spring 1955.
Never mind that one wheel's over
the line.

*Jay Leno on the allure of scooters: "Women come up and go, 'What's that?' You explain it, then you have to explain that you're married."*

• **Sputnik Scooter Club** Oklahoma City's biggest club throws an annual event coordinated with Atomic Brown Scooter Shop. (http://www.sputnikokc.com/)

The other big scooter event in town is Pandora's Box in early October. (http://www.okccuriosity.com)

• **Summit Point** This rally has been running for nearly fifteen years in late September in Virginia, usually in Arrington. (http://www.soulsurvivorsdc.com/summitpoint)

• **Third Coast Rally** Drive around the Spanish missions and look for the basement in the Alamo at this San Antonio, Texas, ride in early November. (http://autos.groups.yahoo.com/group/AlamoScoots/)

• **Tucson-Nogales Fall Classic** While most scooterists in northern climes have safely stored their scooters for the winter, the Pharoahs Scooter Club of Tucson, Arizona, is just getting started for its November rally.

**Scooter Camping**
The Vespa meant freedom, or as Italian rock band Luna Pop chanted, "How beautiful it is to go around with wings under your feet. A Vespa 50 takes away all your problems." As soon as the weekend arrived, Romeo and Giulietta jumped from the balcony to have a picnic.

*"The Salsbury Motor Glide is the greatest woman catcher I have ever seen."*
*—Famous aviator Colonel Roscoe Turner in 1936*

• **Worshipping the Beast** Sponsored by the Burgundy Topz Scooter Club, this long-running event goes through California's capital city, Sacramento, in late September. (http://burgundytopz.com)

**International Rallies**
• **Australian National Scooter Rally** This rally usually takes place in Dubbo, New South Wales, and is one of the larger scooter events down under. (http://www.dubbo2005.com)

• **Paris Scooter Show** There's nothing like fall in the City of Lights, especially atop a vintage Lambretta zooming down the Champs Elysées. (http://www.vulcansc.fr.st)

**STARTING A SCOOTER CLUB**
• **Contact Your Local Scooter Shop:** People have to buy and maintain their scooters somewhere, so your friendly local scooter store knows where the scooters are. Tell the manager to spread the word that

## PUTT-PUTT ODDITIES
## FEZ-TOPPED SHRINERS

In the United States beginning in the 1950s, the scooter show inevitably revolved around the town festival with fez-topped Shriners as the centerpiece, performing dangerously slow figure-eight maneuvers on their Cushman scooters while tossing taffy to the tots. Rockers had their BSAs, Hell's Angels their Harleys, Mods their Lambrettas, and Shriners their Cushmans.

The Masonic pact was signed by Shriner Bill Ammon, son of Cushman's intrepid leader Charles Ammon, who convinced the company to offer a special Shriner scooter in 1957. Leather fringe and shiny rivets also helped show off the steeds as well as chrome widgets including horns, safety bars, floorboards, air shrouds, seat rails, locking gas caps, and fender tips. In an attempt to steal the Masonic market from Cushman, even Vespas were offered with special Shriner accessories.

you're starting a club that meets every week or once a month. The bigger the scooter community, the more sales for the shop. While you're there, pin up a poster for your scooter club.

If you don't have a scooter shop in town, find out where most of your fellow scooterists order their parts. Ask that dealer if there are more scooterists in your area. Perhaps they'll even package flyers for your club with orders that go out to your town.

• **Start a 'Zine, Design a Website:** Newsletters and little photocopied magazines (or 'zines) make members feel like they're part of a community and attract new scooterists. Ask for articles and photos from members, get out the scanner, and print your paper.

'Zines have been mostly replaced by websites because suddenly the whole world can know about your club. Create a logo for your club and feature it prominently on the website. Con your little brother or the computer whiz at the office into designing a website for your club with lots of photos. To help form the community, include a chatroom, a place to list scooters with parts for sale, with links to scooter shops and mechanics.

• **Make Flyers, Make Stickers:** Using that fancy new logo, make a flyer or postcard announcing your scooter club. Post it at your scooter shop, leave them on the seats of scooters you see. If you're truly ambitious, have stickers made of with your club's logo. Some clubs even make slick patches that can be sewed onto jackets.

• **Be Visible:** Park your scooter (locked!) where people can see it. Display your new club sticker boldly on the legshield. When you meet with your club, park in front of the café or bar so the world can see your scoots.

• **Hold Regular Meetings:** With everyone's busy schedule, it's next to impossible to coordinate many people to meet at the same time. Therefore, plan a reoccurring time once a month on a weekend or evening to meet. Having a fixed time will make it simple for everyone to remember when to come, even though some won't be able to show up all the time.

• **Plan a Ride:** Give yourself plenty of time—at least a month or two—to plan your big scooter ride. This will be the big moment of truth when all your club organ-

*Emancipated Scooterist*
When the Lambretta A debuted in 1947, women flocked to the scooter to be freed from *la mamma*'s apron strings. While men had their Moto Guzzis and Laverdas, Italian women wanted a vehicle just for them.

izing will come to fruition. Most importantly, do not be disappointed with a small turn-out. Eventually you and your club members will be able to brag that you were at the first annual event.

• **Keep It Fun:** Remember that people join clubs to be with like-minded people who share a common interest. Don't organize too much. No one wants Robert's Rules of Order dictated to them with presidents and committees (unless you're part of the Italian Vespa Clubs). This is a social event and should be a blast, right?

## A TALE OF TWO CITIES' CLUBS: MILAN'S LAMBRETTA VS. PISA'S VESPA

"Milan is an occupied city," any Italian Lambretta rider will tell you. Not by the Germans from the north, and the Spanish scourge has long since left. Even the Veneziani and the Austro-Hungarian empire have lost their claim. No, no, it's much worse; Milan is occupied by *Vespisti*.

Vespisti is the Italian word for Vespa aficionados. They buzz through the streets on their two-wheeled "wasp" scooters, defying traffic lights and weaving through stalled traffic. They block the sidewalks parking their Pisa-made scooters to avoid any walking, as the police conveniently ignore their audacity—since the fuzz is unable to combat the swarm. This lawlessness is nothing new to Milan. In the old days, however, the blatant scooter violations were committed by the home team, the *Lambrettisti*, and therefore largely overlooked.

The enormous Innocenti factory in the Lambrate section of Milan pumped out

**Wanna drag?**
Is he looking down on the little Vespa or wishing he could catch a ride with the buxom fraulein? With a peppy two-stroke engine, the Vespa could beat any car off the starting line—at least for the first ten feet.

thousands of Lambrettas, which are named for the Lambro river whose waters generously washed away the pollution caused by constructing these glorious scooters. The powerful two-stroke motors once mobilized this war-torn city to become the powerhouse of Italy. For once, Milan could be proud of its homegrown progeny, but that was then ....

During the sluggish 1970s, as scooter sales plummeted and the last Lambrettas exited the Innocenti factory, the menace of scooters made in Pisa prepared their attack.

I went to the annual motorcycle exhibition in the outskirts of Milan to assess the damage. The Lambro river flows near the grounds, but its once dark waters became blacker as companies like Innocenti gave up scooters for automobile production. Now this sad creek has been cleaned up and part of the empty factory which was slated to become a shopping mall has now been torn down.

As I entered the grounds I noticed that most everyone was drooling over classic motorcycles. When I asked a couple of men gazing at a Moto Guzzi where the Lambretta area was, they

laughed, "I thought that scooters weren't allowed in here!"

Ignoring their jovial ignorance, I wandered through the exhibition past the makeshift espresso bar where lines of men dosed up on the steaming brown liquid only to increase their excitement about their beloved motorcycles.

There, raised on a velvet-covered pedestal, was a shining Lambretta: part icon, part defiance against Vespas, but mostly a symbol of inspiration to go fix up those old Innocenti scooters and recall past Milanese glory.

A huge group was gathered around the scooter arguing furiously with arms flailing. As I approached, the crowd became instantly silent and every head turned to check me out. My friend Vittorio came out from the crowd and told them, "It's OK, he's one of us."

They nodded towards me and resumed their discussion. Today's topic/argument was the perennial discussion of the supposed superiority of the older, uncovered Lambrettas compared to the later "sheathed" scooters. While lines

## HOLY VESPA!:
## THE SCOOTER BODY OF CHRIST

Talk of the scooter as savior didn't seem to bother the Holy See. In fact, the millionth Vespa was brought to an altar and officially blessed by the Vatican. The Church saw the scooter as a means for the masses to get to mass on time. Much to the Vatican's delight, *Time* reported in 1956, "More people were baptized in 1955 [and] more went to Communion this Easter than ever in history. One reason: motor scooters." The article went on to say:

"Pope Pius XII has been a longtime friend of automation; last fall he called for 'greater and greater speed to the glory of God.' Priests in Italy, according to a Vatican report, currently own 30,850 motorscooters, and in terms of sacraments and good works, the average priest's efficiency has climbed to about 3,000% over that of his road-trudging 19th century predecessor. Another straw in this high wind is the decline of the more introverted Benedictines and foot-slogging Franciscans in favor of the fast-moving Jesuits, whose high-octane practicality thrives on the motor-scooter age."

Life magazine rebutted this slam of Franciscans, however, in 1957 with a photo of a Capucin "Brother Henry" zooming down Baltic Street in Brooklyn on his Vespa with sidecar pulling a roller skater.

The Vatican continues to give thanks to the wonderful Vespa. Pope John Paul II twice had an audience with the president of the Fédération Internationale des Vespa Clubs, Christa Solbach, and gave his papal blessing to scooterists the world over.

---

were being drawn in the carpet, a few Lambrettisti approached me introducing themselves under their breath as though not wanting to have anyone else overhear exactly who they are.

Stefano, the editor of *Scooter* magazine, gave me a few copies of his publication, in which there was a curious shortage of Vespas. When I asked about it, he told me, "Nobody is *really* interested in them. People just put up with them since there are more Vespas made than any other Italian scooter."

Meanwhile, Vittorio, who had set up the impressive Lambretta display, joined us. He glared at the grandiose Vespa Club di Milano display occupying the center of the largest tent, and asked rhetorically, "Why should they get the prime spot with all that space? And look, there's no one even there!"

When I told them that I was going to take some photos of the Vespas for a scooter book, Stefano told me to ask them how they got the best area in the tent. I felt like a scooter spy checking out the competition. When I asked them if they wanted to join me, they just shrugged as though they'd seen all that stuff before. They bid me well as I crossed enemy lines.

More than a dozen scooters formed a large, red-carpeted aisle to the center area where a couple of well-dressed Vespa bureaucrats stood in front of a huge banner declaring their simple mantra, "Vespa!!!" I remembered the copy of an old German Vespa ad that suddenly had new meaning, "Über alle ist Vespaland." (Obvious scooter propaganda.)

In spite of the luxurious display of ribbons, banners, and trophies, Vittorio was right, the crowd was noticeably missing. Even though they staked claim to the largest, most prominent area—while most displays were allowed space for only two or three vehicles—they still couldn't lure converts to their power base.

As I approached the empty walkway between the two lines of scooters, I wasn't sure if I could just walk onto the red carpet and whip off some snapshots. One of the prim, name-tagged Vespisti with his arms behind his back walked purposely back and forth as though guarding his line of the scooters. When he noticed my approach, he greeted me immediately, grabbing my hand from my side and shaking it profusely, exclaiming, *"Buon giorno,* I'm Marco." He was obviously thrilled to have someone pay attention to their impressive assortment of classic Vespas. He encouraged me to take photos and spoke ad nauseam about the history of each prestigious scooter and their honorable owners.

Just then, I was asked to move aside as an Armani-clad man walked up the aisle to

### Scooter Badges

Once the scooter club is formed and role call taken, a membership badge is required to plaster on the legshield. Each year a new sticker or patch is designed for the annual ride. This collection is proudly displayed at the scooter museum in Rudesheim, Germany.

his position at the head of the display. Marco became noticeably nervous when he walked by and whispered to me that the man is the president of the Vespa Club di Milano. When he sat down, a couple other Vespisti at the table immediately engaged him in conversation.

Marco told me, "Since you have come all the way from the United States to see our display, you should really meet our esteemed leader." Before I could tell him that I didn't really have anything to say to the president, I was grabbed by the arm and whisked over to him. I waited for a few minutes for the president's attention and realized that Marco would never interrupt the conversation going on, so I cut in and introduced myself.

The president said, "People visit us from all over the world. After all, we are one of the largest and most important Vespa clubs in the world." He insisted that I attend one of the weekly Vespa meetings where they discuss the merits and marvels of Vespa scooters.

I told him that I would like that, and realized that it was time to pose the treasonous question. "How come the Vespa Club di Milano was given the largest and most prestigious area, when the Lambretta club was given an area just a quarter the size?"

He looked at me almost in disbelief and said, "Well, as you can see we have the largest display and the most scooters; therefore the Vespa is the most important scooter. Is it not true?" I shrugged noncommittally, not willing to argue with his circular logic. In an attempt to appease him, I promised I'd attend a club meeting.

Instead of returning to my compatriots at the Lambretta display and further fanning the flames of scooter rivalry, I headed for the coffee bar. All the Lambrettisti were getting more wired on shots of espresso, so I couldn't avoid being a double agent and revealing what the Vespa club president had said. I don't know whether their faces grew red out of anger or the caffeine flowing through their veins had taken effect. Regardless, I didn't wait

*Lambretta on a Pedestal*
**At a motorcycle show outside of Milan, this Lambretta was featured prominently. "I thought that scooters weren't allowed in here!" joked a thick-headed motorcyclist. The Vespa Club di Milano claimed an enormous space, however, compared to the one lone Lambretta Series II (pictured) as the Milanese competition to the ubiquitous Vespa of Pisa.**

around to find out and escaped before a scooter rumble erupted.

## THE MILLIONTH VESPA

In April 1956, the one-millionth Vespa was produced, combining all factories in France, England, Germany, and elsewhere that were building Vespas under license. A celebration was held in Pontedera and Vespa Day was declared throughout Italy, with festivities held in 15 Italian cities, including a convoy of 2,000 Vespas traveling en masse through Rome and halting all traffic. The Piaggio factory in Italy now manufactured 500 scooters a day, and by this time, the French Vespa firm, ACMA, had produced a total of 100,000 Vespas.

*"As you well know, we are a movement based exclusively on goodness, with none of the poison of political hatred, none of the rigidity of hazy or unreachable idealism; a movement that comes about, expresses itself, and breeds to the beat of small engines and hearts serene...."*
*—Renato Tassinari speaking at the 10th Annual Congress of the Vespa Club d'Italia*

# MOTORSCOOTER MEDIA

**Chapter 8**

## WHAT YOU WILL LEARN

- How to verb "Vespa" and make a noun out of "Lambretta"
- That a poet kept wolves at bay all night by revving his Vespa
- About the greatest scooter movies to hit the silver screen
- How the scooter became a canvas for surrealist Salvador Dali
- The best scooter books ever
- How scooter ads borrowed Pop Art motifs and vice versa

**Lock Up Your Daughters!**
What could be worse than seeing your sweet daughter abducted by a smiling Vespa rider with a pudding basin helmet? Where's Marlon Brando when you need him? This B-movie hit the big screen with wholesome adventurers who dutifully wrapped their sleeping bags in practical plastic and had picnics in the hills.

Mention "motorscooter in a movie" and two films spring to mind (depending on your generation). Older folks wax nostalgic about Audrey Hepburn on the back of Gregory Peck's bulbous Vespa in *Roman Holiday*. William Wyler directed this classic in 1953 and started a revolution for scooters and tourists itching to see the beautiful life in Rome for themselves. (*Three Coins in a Fountain* tried to catch the same feeling but went awry when the short-sighted director failed to include a scooter.)

The other movie that exemplifies the scooter is *Quadrophenia*, which set off a different kind of revolution. The angry, confused Mod named Jimmy rides his Lambretta with a vengeance in search of a better life. Pete Townshend shreds his guitar with his bowling-ball strums as Roger Daltry screams the tune for the soundtrack. The year that punk rock broke on to the scene—1979—also saw this Mod revival film of the battle of Brighton revisited, and suddenly Johnny Rotten looked like a rebellious dilettante.

Ask the Italians about Vespas on film and two different films will pop to mind that, once again, show the generational split on scooters. The younger set worship the philosopher-cum-director Nanni Moretti as he putts around Rome on his Vespa in *Caro Diario* and just happens to meet Jennifer Beals from *Flashdance* as herself. The scooter provides the vehicle for his train of thoughts in this heady (if sometimes tiresome) film of self discovery.

The older generation of Italians will remember the greatest movie ever shot in Rome, *La Dolce Vita*, with a phalanx of circling scooters tormenting VIPs. Federico Fellini used the buzzing, annoying Vespa to personify the shameless persistence of the media hounds who won't leave the bereaved alone. The image of photographer Paparazzo blinding his prey with magnesium flashbulbs became indelibly engraved on the collective

mind and produced a new word in many languages: "paparazzi." The protagonist newsman Marcello Mastroianni kept Paparazzo as a fair-weather friend as Mastroianni zoomed around in his Lancia Spider and slept with movie stars in prostitutes' beds. Taking place in seven days for the seven hills of Rome, *La Dolce Vita* shows Marcello's existential search—and ultimate failure—for meaning through the sweet indulgence and decadence that Italy has to offer.

## PUTT-PUTT MOVIES: SCOOTS ON THE SILVER SCREEN

Both Piaggio and Innocenti struggled to get their scooters on the screen as product placement next to glamorous stars. Vespa scored with William Wyler's *Roman Holiday* in 1953 and soon after with Cliff Richard on a Vespa in the summer lovin' *Wonderful Life*. Innocenti was not to be left behind and convinced Richard to appear the following year in a teenie bopper flick called *Summer Holiday*—as long as a Lambretta was at his side.

Piaggio probably wasn't thrilled when Vespas were the bandits' scooter of choice in *Les Tricheurs* (The Cheaters), directed by Marcel Carné in 1958. Wild bebop accompanied the doomed rebels zooming down Saint-Germain-des Prés in Paris on their buzzing Vespas. In another scandalous

*"At the moment we're hero-worshipping the Spades—they can dance and sing . . ."*

*—A Mod quoted in 1964 in the book Generation X by Hamblett and Deverson*

# It's Twice-Time!

*Coked-Up Lammie*
In 1968, Coca-Cola took sides in the Vespa-Lambretta wars and this Slimline took the cake as the ultimate Mod machine of the time.

film, leggy Angie Dickinson jumped atop a Vespa in the 1962 *Jessica* as an American midwife who excites the married men of Sicily, so the Italian women resolve to abstain from sex to keep her off their doorstep.

To clean up its image, Piaggio let a 180 SS Vespa be customized with a complete cowling covering the scooter, helicopter sails above, and fins to be able to dive underwater in the movie *Dick Smart 2007*. Franco Prosperi directed this 1967 film as a family-friendly, gadget-centered James Bond on a Super Sport scooter rather than an Aston Martin DB5. The view of the good-natured clown on a scooter persisted for Piaggio, however, as George Lucas chose a Vespa GS 160 to be driven by Terry "Toad" Fields to Mel's Drive-In in *American Graffiti* from 1973.

Vespa easily topped Lambretta with the most film credits: *Racconti d'Estate*

(Tales of Summer) by Gianni Franciolini, *Primo Amore* (First Love) by Mario Camerini, *Mia Nonna Poliziotto*, Federico Fellini's *La Dolce Vita*, *L'Avventura*, *The Talented Mr. Ripley*, *Bounce*, *An American in Paris*, *Absolute Beginners*, *Of Love and Shadows*, *The Conversation*, *American Pie*, *Austin Powers*, *The Wedding Planner*, *Professor Nachtfalter*, and many more.

However, Lambretta can claim the mantle of the movie that defined modern scooterdom: *Quadrophenia* from 1979, with Sting as Ace Face and the best soundtrack of any scooter movie.

## SALVADOR DALI: VESPA SIGNATURE MODEL

Just as Pablo Picasso is credited with painting the first camouflage in a precursor to his cubist vision, so is fellow Spaniard Salvador Dali recognized as the first to sign the right side panel of a Vespa. Perhaps riding on the furor raised when Marcel Duchamp signed a urinal with a pseudonym and declared this "ready made" piece of porcelain a piece of art, Dali took the Vespa design of Corradino D'Ascanio and made it his own in a flagrant act of comic plagiarism. To mock the art world, Salvador Dali notoriously signed dozens of unpainted canvasses for amateur painters to create their own "original" Dali. Unfortunately, Piaggio never jumped on the bandwagon to create a Dada/Surrealist scooter of Dali's own design.

## VESPA IN ADS:
## SCOOTERS SELL BIG MACS

Piaggio's ad campaigns from the 1950s and 1960s drew on the paintings of Rauschenberg, Lichtenstein's pop art, and cheesecake American pin-up paintings from World War II. After years of steady promotion of its brand (and defeating the rival Lambretta in the process), the Vespa was finally considered an icon of cool by the 1980s. Old ads, shop manuals, signage, and anything else bearing the name "Vespa" was suddenly collectible.

When Piaggio launched its second invasion of the United States, no wonder even Mattel put the painfully skinny Barbie atop a Vespa with racing stripes on her helmet. Poor Ken was relegated to ride sidesaddle on the pillion.

Today Vespa overexposure in store windows, magazine ads, and TV spots has suddenly rendered the marque more of a marketing scheme than a badge of honor. Here are some of the worst offenders that use the Vespa to sell everything from potato chips to computer chips: Absolut Vodka, American Express, Banana Republic, Coca-Cola, Dell, Ferrari, Keds, Lexus, McDonald's, Microsoft, Payless Shoes, Pringles, Target, and Timex.

## SCOOTER SLICKS: MAGAZINES FOR HIGHER LEARNING

While underground scooter 'zines and newsletters come and go, glossy magazines endure the ups and downs of scooter interest. On their putt-putt-filled pages of magazines from *Scooter World* to *Scooter*, scooter aficionados herald their affection for these two-stroke wonders and offer advice to those in need.

- **Scootering.** This mainstay of British scooting withstood any slump in interest in the 1980s and 1990s. Obviously this slick publication caters mostly to the U.K. audience with in-depth columns and helpful ads, but can be found at larger magazine stores throughout the United States.

- **Scoot Quarterly.** This 'zine was started by Casey Earls and Barry Synoground from San Francisco in 1998 as a U.S. version of *Scootering* with more focus

*ANNÉE · N· 7 — MENSUEL — NOVEMBRE 1952
76 PAGES COMPTE RENDU COMPLET DU SALON 120 FR.

le Scooter

*Scooter à la Française*
This monthly French scooter mag gave the run down of the latest two-strokes at the 1952 Salon de Paris to help confused customers choose between everything from the Moto Guzzi Galletto to France's own Guiller. Scooters were just beginning their heyday and outrageous designs filled the floor of the Salon. Many of the makes were prototypes, unfortunately, and never made it to the production line.

## TWO-STROKE DIVAS:
### LIMO-LESS VIPs

During the golden age of automobiles, Tinseltown stars risked ridicule by hopping on a little scooter to enjoy southern California outside of the sardine-mobiles clogging the freeways. Away from the limousine, stars could be mobbed when they exposed themselves to their admirers atop only two-wheels.

Some were braver than others, like Paul Newman who famously zoomed around Israel on a Vespa when he shot *Exodus* in 1960. The future race car driver deemed the Vespa too dangerous for his wife Joanne Woodward to do the same. Many well-known stars called the scooter their own, including Jean-Paul Belmondo, May Britt, Charlie Chaplin, Bobby Darin, Sandra Dee, Henry Fonda, Audrey Hepburn, Charlton Heston, William Holden, Gina Lollobrigida, Jayne Mansfield, Dean Martin (Dino Crocetti), Gregory Peck, Anthony Perkins, Anthony Quinn, Jacques Sernas, Sting, Mamie Van Doren, John Wayne, Raquel Welch, and Natalie Wood.

In an attempt to capture some of the class that Gregory Peck bestowed upon the humble scooter, these modern movie stars now pose for paparazzi on their new scoots, hoping that the some of the cool will rub off: Kirstie Alley, Marc Anthony, Sandra Bullock, Matthew Broderick, Robert De Niro, Vin Diesel, Kirsten Dunst, Carrie Fisher, Flea, Wayne Gretsky, Lenny Kravitz, Matt Lauer, Jude Law, Jay Leno, Gwyneth Paltrow, Sarah Jessica Parker, Jerry Seinfeld, Steven Spielberg, and Sylvester Stallone.

on stock, classic bikes. Scooter scene reports are drawn and published from across the country—and the globe. In 2003, Earls and Synoground sold *Scoot* to fellow collaborators, but the magazine persists in its vision of reviewing classic and modern scooters.

## SCOOTER BOOKS

The past 15 years has seen a boom in scooter publications, but so many have been snatched up by hungry readers that some have gone out of print and are only available secondhand for a tidy fee. Here's a nearly complete list of reading to keep the true scooter buff busy for years.

*Mods!* Barnes, Richard. London: Eel Pie Publishing, 1979. Full of black and white photos that capture the feeling of the time like no other book. Highly recommended (if you can find it). Also check out the companion book *Rockers!* to get the whole bipartisan view.

*Brum Brum: 254,000 Chilometri in Vespa.* Bettinelli, Giorgio. Milan: Feltrinelli, 2002.

*Vespa . . . e Tutti i Suoi Vespini.* Biancalana, Stefano and Marchianò, Michele. *La* Vimodrone (Milan): Giorgio Nada Editore, 1995.

*Il Libro Della Comunicazione.* Boldrini, Maurizio and Calabrese, Omar. Pontedera: Piaggio Veicoli Europei S.p.A. 1995.

*Vespa: An Illustrated History.* Brockway, Eric. Sparkford, England: Haynes Publications, 1993.

*The Cult of the Vespa.* Calabrese, Omar. Pontedera: Piaggio Veicoli Europei S.p.A. 1996.

*Lambretta Innocenti: An Illustrated History.* Cox, Nigel. Sparkford, England: Haynes Publications, 1996.

*Illustrated MotorScooter Buyer's Guide.* Dregni, Michael and Eric. Osceola, Wisconsin: Motorbooks International, 1993. Also published in German.

*Scooters!* Dregni, Michael and Eric. Osceola, Wisconsin: Motorbooks International, 1995. Out-of-print.

*Scooter Mania!* Dregni, Eric. Osceola, Wisconsin: Motorbooks International, 1998. Out-of-print.

*Scooter Bible.* Dregni, Michael & Eric. Center Conway, New Hampshire: Whitehorse Press, 2005. A compilation of *Illustrated MotorScooter Buyer's Guide* and *Scooters!* in full-color as a coffee table book.

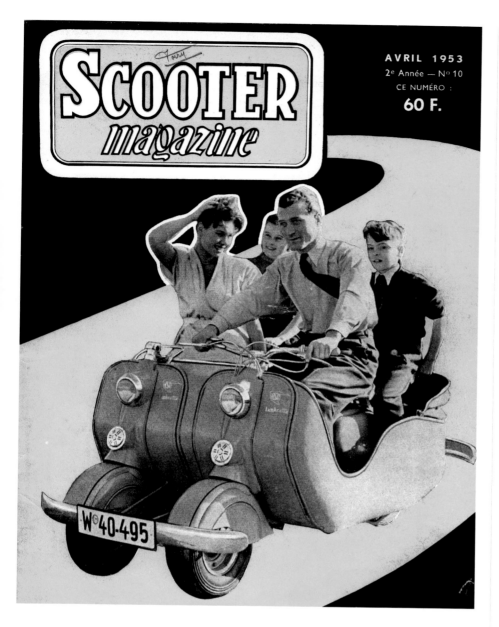

SCOOTER *magazine*

AVRIL 1953
2e Année — N° 10
CE NUMÉRO :
60 F.

W 40-495

*NSU's Scooter Car*
**France's *Scooter Magazine* splashed the outrageous NSU Lambretta car across the front cover in 1953. The scooter on four wheels was only a gimmick prototype/project scooter that was used for promotion and never went into production.**

*Scooters du Monde: 100 Ans d'Histoire.* Dumas, François-Marie and Didier, Ganneau. Paris: Éditions E/P/A, 1995. Excellent book all in French. Uncovers the Gallic history of scooters previously unknown to the Italo-centric scooter scribes.

*Una Leggenda Verso il Futuro: I Centodieci Anni di Storia della Piaggio.* Fanfani, Tommaso. Pontedera: Piaggio Veicoli Europei, 1994.

*Mustang: A Different Breed of Steed.* Gerald, Michael. N.p.: self-published, n.d.

*Tous les Scooters du Monde.* Goyard, Jean and Pascal, Dominique. Paris: Éditions Ch. Massin, 1988.

*Vespa Histoire et Technique.* Goyard, Jean; Pascal, Dominique; and Salvat, Bernard. Paris Éditions Moto Legende/Rétroviseur, 1992.

"Punti dalla Vespa" *Specchio della Stampa.* Gramellini, M. and Calabrese, Omar. (February 24, 1996).

"Object as Image: The Italian Scooter Cycle" from *Hiding in the Light.* Hebdige, Dick. London and New York: Routledge, 1988. This essay can also be found in *The Consumer Society Reader* from Blackwell Publishers, 2000. Hebdige is painfully smart and essential reading for the philosophically minded. Understand your scooter lust and history by reading this essay.

*Ursula Andress*
Helping to make the Vespa the ultimate Mod accessory on Carnaby Street, Ursula Andress pushed her Piaggio in the 1965 calendar. Surprisingly, this shot didn't make the cut for the calendar.

*Deutsche Motorroller 1949–73.* Kubisch, Ulrich, ed. München, Germany: Scrader Automobil-Bücher, 1992.

*Vespa Mi'amore.* Kubisch, Ulrich. Hösseringen, Germany: Schrader Verlag, 1993.

*Lambretta Story* (video cassette). Milan, Italy: Giorgio Nada, 1994.

*Deutsche Roller und Kleinwagen der Fünfziger Jahre.* Lintelmann, Reinhard. Brilon, Germany: Podszun Motor-Bücher, 1986.

*Vespa: Style in Motion.* Mazzanti, Davide. San Francisco: Chronicle Books, 2004.

*Absolute Beginners.* MacInnes, Colin. Allison and Busby, reprint in 1980.

*Scooters de Chez Nous.* Pascal, Dominique. Boulogne, France: Éditions MDM, 1993.

*Empire Made: The Handy Parka Pocket Guide to All Things Mod!* Rawlings, Terry and Badman, Keith. London: Complete Music Publications, 1997. Hard to get, but essential reading for the true Mod. Very British and very tongue-in-cheek.

*Chi Vespa Mangia le Mele: Storia della Vespa.* Rivola, Luigi. Milano: Giorgio Nada Editore: 1993.

*Vespa Bella Donna.* Roos, Peter. Kiel, Germany: Nieswand Verlag, 1990. Good looking book with lots of glossy photos.

*Vespa Stracciatella: Ein Lust und Bilderbuch von der Italienischen Beweglichkeit.* Roos, Peter. Berlin: Transit Buchverlag, 1985.

*Poet on a Scooter.* Roskolenko, Harry. New York: Dial Press, 1958. Very well-written book about an American poet who sets out from Paris alone on an around-the-world adventure. Recommended.

"All Around the World on a Scooter," from *Solo: The Great Adventures Alone.* Roskolenko, Harry. Chicago: Playboy Press, 1973.

*Scooters: Red Eyes, Whitewalls and Blue Smoke.* Shattuck, Colin and Peterson, Eric. Denver: Speck Press, 2005. Brand new, well-designed book that focuses on clubs, rallies, and the modern (classic) scooter scene.

*A History of the Cushman Eagle.* Somerville, Bill. Ponca City, Okla.: Cushman Pub., n.d.

*A History of the Cushman Motor Works.* Somerville, Bill. Ponca City, Okla.: Cushman Pub., 1986.

*Allstate Scooters & Cycles 1951–1961.* Somerville, Bill. Ponca City, Okla.: Cushman Pub., 1990.

*The Complete Guide to Cushman Motor Scooters.* Somerville, Bill. Ponca City, Okla.: Cushman Pub., 1988.

*Motor Scooters Colour Family Album.* Sparrow, Andrea and David. Dorchester, UK: Veloce Publishing Plc., 1998.

*Vespa Colour Family Album.* Sparrow, Andrea and David. Dorchester, UK: Veloce Publishing Plc., 1995.

**Eating Road Apples**
The most famous Vespa publicity campaign was ripe with innuendo. "Whoever rides a Vespa eats the apples," made youngsters who had diligently studied the Bible at school in Catholic Italy giggle with glee thinking of that naughty Eve and the do-gooder Adam. Nevertheless, even priests putted around atop Vespas—except those holier-than-thou Franciscans who preferred poverty and eating exhaust while trudging along in their brown robes.

## VERBING VESPA:
### EATING EDEN'S APPLE

Ad execs in the Piaggio boardroom realized that driving atop a two-stroke meant more than just a trip to town. The Vespa set Italian teenagers free from the shackles of mama and papà and allowed them to mingle with their peers in the piazza. More than this, though, the scooter as two-seated matchmaker let these hormone-crazed youngsters taste the sweet fruits of youth.

Serpentine advertisers knew their Vespa would throw Italy out of the puritanical garden of yesteryear and their publicity posters bragged, "*Chi 'Vespa' mangia le mele (chi non 'Vespa' no)*." The famous ad translated as "Whoever 'Vespas' eats the apples, (whoever doesn't 'Vespa' doesn't)," and in one fell swoop verbed the word 'Vespa' and promised a bite from the tree of knowledge. Sin and sex—everything the modern teenager wanted—could be had behind the handlebars of the Vespa. Catholic Italy would never be the same.

The tongue-in-cheek campaign continued with apple symbolism, but Piaggio was careful to avoid having any Eve-like beauty eating the fruit for fear of upsetting the devout. Instead, cryptic ads told Vespa riders to eat "the daisy apple in the meadows," "the heart apple with one's partner," "the star apple with your headlights on," and "the green apple with your head held high." The verbing of Vespa used more direct innuendo beyond just "If you Vespa..." to "*Vespizzatevi!*" ("Get Vespa-ed!").

Piaggio's home factory is located in Tuscany and in the local dialect, *mela* (apple) means buttocks—a fact surely not lost on its advertisers since the apple in their ads was especially plump and bulbous.

in tutto il mondo

*Vespa*

*In the Whole World...*
While Piaggio ran constant ads to persuade more scooterists (mostly from buying a Lambretta), the best publicity was word of mouth through scooter clubs and the ubiquitous Vespa zooming through town. Before the term "product placement" came into use, Vespas were projected on the silver screen underneath super stars like Gregory Peck and Marcello Mastroianni turning the humble Vespa into a new Italian icon.

*Vespa*. Struss, Dieter. Augsburg: Battenberg Verlag, 1995.

*Rockers!* Stuart, Johnny. London: Plexus Publishing Ltd. 1987. The companion book to *Mods!*

*Innocenti Lambretta*. Tessera, Vittorio. Vimodrone (Milan): Giorgio Nada Editore, 1995. Translated into English as well. This hefty hardcover from "Mr. Lambretta" (Vittorio Tessera) covers all the models and complete history of the beloved Lambretta.

*Scooters Made in Italy.* Tessera, Vittorio. Vimodrone (Milan): Giorgio Nada Editore, 1993. Tessera draws from his exten-sive scooter archives to show all the unusual makes from Italy. In Italian only and rather difficult to find. Perhaps only available at Giorgio Nada's automotive bookstore (Libreria dell'Automobile) in Milan.

*Vespa Story* (video cassette). Milan, Italy: Giorgio Nada Editore, 1992. Interviews with Corradino D'Ascanio are the highlight along with archival footage of Piaggio.

*Vespa Timesurfer* (CD-ROM). Pontedera: Fondazione Piaggio, 1994.

*Scooterama: Café Chic and Urban Cool.* Walker, Alastair. London: Carlton Books Ltd., 1999.

*Musical Vespas*
After a hearty portion of haggis, this scooterist can't resist blowing a tune on his bagpipes to entertain fellow Vespisti at the rally. Notice no one has hung around for the Scottish serenade.

*Motor Scooters.* Webster, Michael. Haverfordwest, England: Shire Publications, Ltd., 1986. Essentially the first booklet chronicling the wide range of bizarre scooters. Highly recommended, but unfortunately it's rather slim.

*The Scooter Book.* Woods, Bob. Irvington, New York: Hylas Publishing, 2004. Mostly new scooters with a tip of the hat to old scooters. Not as cutting edge or weird as one would hope (perhaps because

it's written by a motorcyclist).

*Vespa Motorroller 1948-1986.* Zeichner, Walter, ed. München, Germany: Schrader Automobil-Bücher, 1987.

## MOD LIT: ABSOLUTE BEGINNERS

More than any other book, Colin MacInnes' *Absolute Beginners* from 1959 captures the spirit of Soho and Carnaby Street in London at the birth of the Mod movement.

"You could see everywhere the

**Lambrettability**
If Piaggio can verb "Vespa," why can't Innocenti make a noun of Lambretta? This British ad appealed to the English desire to be rid of the rain and lie on the beach. Never mind that when the young Modernists on their Lambrettas went to Brighton they threw beach chairs at the Rockers on their BSAs.

signs of the un-silent teenage revolution. The disc shops with those lovely sleeves set in their windows and the kids inside them purchasing guitars or spending fortunes on the songs of the Top Twenty. The shirt-stores and bra-stores with cine-star photos in their windows, selling exclusive teenage drag…. Scooters and bubble-cars driven madly down the roads by kids, who, a few years ago, were pushing toy ones on the pavement."

### HARRY ROSKOLENKO: VESPA KEEPS THE WOLVES AT BAY

Setting out from Paris to New York (via Kolhapur and Kalgoorlie), poet Harry Roskolenko made one of the first round the world trips on a scooter beginning on January 3, 1956. "I would be king of the

Scooters make great canvases upon which to display popular artwork.

Thirtysix victories in the Sporting world in 1948. of the F. I. C. M. International Motorcycle trophy the silver Medal at the six-day International

*"We say that the world's magnificence has been enriched by a new beauty; the beauty of speed."*
—F.T. Marinetti in his *Futurist Manifesto*, which inspired a generation of Italians to search for faster planes, trains, and scooters.

scooter, an emperor of ruts, the prince of the open country and the servant of my own eyes and spirit," Roskolenko wrote enthusiastically on his departure. As a sort of *Zen and the Art of Motorcycle Maintenance* for the scooter, *Poet on a Scooter* is graphic, erudite, and philosophical in spite of various old time, hard-drinking beat poet clichés such as, "A blond Dutch girl, frail of morals but firm of breasts, drank too much and cried."

He describes Iran as the land of opium and nearly gets "temporarily married" to a Persian virgin *sigheh* for a few days. "I would intone words like *zuwwujtku, ankuhooku, muttvatoku,* meaning, 'I have married thee temporarily.' And so I waited, wondering if this seductive session that Mme. Pars was arranging would keep me

More than fiftythousand Vespa in circulation on the roads of Italy and of 35 foreign Nations

*Because* helps the clerk and the functionary to shorten the distances between their homes and their offices.

*Because* during week-end trips permits the discovery of charming places in the country, at the sea side and in the mountains, and makes for marvellous holidays.

*Because* helps the field Representative to visit more customers per day, thus increasing his selling capacity.

...THE *Vespa* 125cc. IS THE MOST LARGELY DISTRIBUTED MOTOR SCOOTER IN THE WORLD...

forever in Iran, my Vespa scooter rusting to the color of an ancient camel."

Apart from his salacious Arabian nights, Roskolenko also has his near-death experiences. "One night, in the high mountains of Turkish Kurdistan, I used my Vespa engine to fight off a pack of wolves . . . aiming the scooter's exhaust out toward the pack, again I started the motor, revving it up and exploding it like a machine gun. I had found a weapon, a powerful noisemaker, but a weapon which could kill me too with its fumes. It exploded its furies whenever I revved it up—but what if the spark plug fouled or the fuel ran out? . . . With the

scooter's exhaust holding the wolves at bay, I stood there, thinking, praying, freezing yet soaked in sweat, and when the fumes became too strong, I cut the motor down for a few moments, peering at the pack through the darkness to judge their reaction, listening to their howling, then revving, revving, revving, revving, all through the four-letter night."

With his Vespa as the co-star for the victorious raid around the world, Roskolenko writes at the end of the trip, "I had spent ninety-seven dollars on fuel. I had traveled 37,000 miles, 21,000 of them by scooter, on the folkways and byways of the world."

*Vespa Ad*

**How many more reasons are needed to get yourself "Vespa'd"? The earliest Vespas put Italy back on its feet after its factories were flattened by Allied bombers, but soon families could afford a car and mom or junior took over the family scooter. By the 1960s and 1970s, scooters were deemed more of a teenager gadabout and the bottom fell out of the market.**

# SCOOTER SPEAK

**Glossary**

**BENCH SEAT:** Long, two-person seat.

**BLISTERHEAD:** Insult to scooterists who wear pudding basin helmets. Sometimes called "bubbleheads."

**BUBBLEHEAD:** See "blisterhead."

**CAFÉ RACER:** Souped-up motorcycle ridden by Rockers. These bikes had low handlebars and were usually British bikes, especially BSA, Royal Enfield, Triumph, and Norton.

**LA DOLCE VITA:** Italian for "the sweet life," a film featuring Paparazzo on a Vespa.

**DOODLEBUG:** Synonym for scooter. However, Beam named its miniature scooter the Doodlebug in 1946.

**DUSTBIN:** Derogatory term for scooter, usually refers to the oversized Maico Mobile, however.

**FOUR-STROKE:** An engine that burns the gas and oil separately and more efficiently than a two-stroke. Several modern scooters are four-stroke along with a couple of vintage scooters. Most scooters use peppy two-stroke engines for more speed and lower-end torque.

**GYMKHANA:** A scooter obstacle course. Believed to have been born in British-controlled India by Bengali lancers for battle training.

**ITALIAN HAIR DRYER:** Pejorative Rocker term for Italian scooters, especially Vespas and Lambrettas.

**LAMMIE:** Short for Lambretta. Sometimes spelled "Lambie."

**LAMBRETTISTA:** Lambretta rider and aficionado. Can be masculine or feminine. Plural is *Lambrettisti*.

**MAXI-SCOOTER:** The new breed of enormous scooters usually with a reclined seat, excess of 200-cc engine, and plenty of plastic. The Honda Helix was the original barcalounger scooter, but has been surpassed by the 582-cc Honda Silver Wing and the 650-cc Suzuki Burgman.

**MOD:** Short for Modern or Modernist. A style and subculture sprouting in England and espousing Italian style, scooters, and fast living. Mods were the die-hard enemies of Rockers in 1960s England. (See Chapter 5)

**MOPED**: A motorized bicycle with a 50-cc engine or less that rarely exceeds 30 miles per hour. Usually does not need a driver's license to be driven. Also a pointed insult towards the ride of any self-respecting scooterist.

**PAPARAZZO**: Marcello Mastroianni's photographer sidekick in *La Dolce Vita* who rode a buzzing Vespa through the star-studded Via Veneto and shamelessly shot photos for a Roman newspaper. The name became synonymous with photography leeches and usually used in the plural: paparazzi.

**PILLION**: Rear seat on a scooter that is usually just a square, covered pad without a back rest.

**PILLION FODDER**: Misogynist term for girlfriend on the back seat of the scooter.

**POWERED ROLLER-SKATE**: Derogatory nickname for early scooters, probably by envious motorcyclists.

**PUDDING BASIN**: Half-sphere helmet that has no chin guard and usually doesn't have a face mask.

**PUDDLE-JUMPERS**: Nickname for early scooters. Now this term is mostly used for small-engined airplanes.

**PUTT-PUTT**: Early term for scooter because of the noise of the two-stroke engine.

**RADUNO**: Italian for rally.

**RAID**: A long trip with a group of scooterists. Often endurance races across country.

**ROCKER**: Motorcyclists, especially from 1960s England, who listened to early rock-n-roll, dressed in American cowboy-inspired style with greased-back hair, and fought the Mods on the beaches of Brighton.

**RUDE BOY**: Angry Rocker, especially punks.

**SADDLE SEAT**: Single seat (similar to old bicycle seats).

**SHARK SKIN**: Sleek material used especially for Italian suits that gives off a two-tone shimmer in the light.

**SKA**: Upbeat Jamaican music style popular with Mod revivalists in the 1970s and 1980s.

**SNAKE**: A line of scooters, particularly when winding up mountain switchbacks.

**TED**: Short for Teddy Boy. A British style similar to the Dandies.

**TWIST 'N GO**: An automatic scooter with no clutch or gearbox and therefore easier to drive for the beginner.

**TWO-TONE**: Two-color paint job.

**TWO-STROKE**: An engine that burns the gas and oil together with a two-part process, as opposed to four-stroke engines that are generally used in larger motors. Most scooters use two-stroke engines, which are generally more fuel efficient than four-strokes, but tend to pollute more. Two-stroke engines generally have more pep and are faster off the line.

**VESPISTA**: Vespa rider and aficionado. Can be masculine or feminine. Plural is *Vespisti*.

**VESPISTICO**: Adjective of Vespa. For example, "rally vespistico" means a Vespa rally.

**VESPIZZARE**: To ride a Vespa. Sometimes is simply "to vespa." Also used in the reflexive: *Vespizzarsi* (to get Vespa-ed) and conjugated as a command: *Vespizzati!* or *Vespizzatevi!* (get yourself/selves Vespa-ed).

**VEST-POCKET MOTORCYCLES**: Early negative nickname for pre-World War II scooters.

**ZOOT SUIT**: Man's suit with padded shoulders and tapered trousers with a narrow cuff. Usually a two-breasted Italian suit with Mafia connotations, but sometimes worn by Mods.

# Index

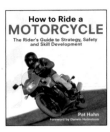

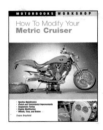
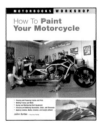